GLIMPSES OF HELL

CHILDHOOD JOURNEY THROUGH CONFUSION, CHAOS AND FEAR

BRENDA RATAJCZAK

Glimpses of Hell
Childhood Journey Through Confusion, Chaos and Fear
All Rights Reserved.
Copyright © 2020 Brenda Ratajczak
v3.0

The opinions expressed in this manuscript are solely the opinions of the author and do not represent the opinions or thoughts of the publisher. The author has represented and warranted full ownership and/or legal right to publish all the materials in this book.

This book may not be reproduced, transmitted, or stored in whole or in part by any means, including graphic, electronic, or mechanical without the express written consent of the publisher except in the case of brief quotations embodied in critical articles and reviews.

Outcry Publishing

Paperback ISBN: 978-0-578-22920-1
Hardback ISBN: 978-0-578-22921-8

Cover Photo © 2019 Brenda Ratajczak. All rights reserved - used with permission.

PRINTED IN THE UNITED STATES OF AMERICA

Glimpses of Hell

Childhood Journey Through

Confusion, Chaos and Fear

Written and illustrated by:
Brenda Alice Ratajczak
(Williams-Barnes-Edwards)

---·◆·---

Some of these stories still haunt me, it's true
Some left scars on my heart, quite a few
Each of these stories I wrote took a toll
Challenged my memory, tarnished my soul
When both of your parents are ill in some way
Within the walls of your home there is hell to pay
You can raise up and be better by far
Or you can succumb to the abuse and the scars

---·◆·---

These stories are dark and heartbreaking
These stories were hidden from light
Two lives that were tainted and haunted
Two little girls fighting for life
These stories are true and foreboding
They caused too much pain to recall
Sixty years hidden and whispered
One sister would rise, one would fall

---·◆·---

Table of Contents

Glimpses of Hell..i
   Prologue to "Glimpses of Hell"..................... iii
   Synopsis v
   Melbalene.. 1
   George 7
   Moonlight Meadow.. 13
   Buckhannon 21
Remembrance... 29
   Sewickley Valley 30
   Alone 39
   Together 48
   Damaged.. 58
   Desperate 68
   Violence 80
   Abuse.. 88
   The Runaways 97
   Tales of Marriages and Hospitals 107
Mommy in the Window – 2001 119
   Tales of Alcohol and Crimes 121
Daddy Who... 131
   One Shall Rise 133
For Debbie from Brenda.................................... 142
   One Shall Fall.. 143
Summer (says Sandy) 1963 151
   Facing Past Demons 152

Struggle on the Streets 159
Losing Dad 168
Finding Dad 175
Losing Mom 177
Losing Mom Again 184
Losing Mom 194
Tears and Rain (Sandy says goodbye.) 196
Flowers and Angels (Sandy says goodbye.) 197
Journeys 198
Tribute to a Father – Jim (May 7, 1997) 205
The Dogwood 207

Glimpses of Hell

(Dec 2018)

I'll not write a chapter of the hurt and the pain
That could be a best seller, if I'd visit again
The dark and sad things hid away from the light
That brought terror to sisters and sanity took flight
A father can bring screams, from his little girls' throats
And tears to their eyes when evil he invokes
A mom can cause daughters to cry in the dark
When crazy acts by her illness are sparked
The smell of liquor on a father's foul breath
As he takes from his girls their innocence and worth
Thrown in a closet by a mother gone mad
For hours on end is far beyond sad
The stories are endless the plot is so cruel
But the worst part about it, it would all be true
Damage of a lifetime will not take book form
And "Glimpses of Hell" will not cause others alarm
I'll not open a way for evil to pass through
By reliving the past, no matter how true
I've laid this to rest such a long time ago
As are the players, the leads in this show
They've both left this world, my dad and my mom
I've forgiven both for the shock and the harm
I'm sure at some point evil will take a stand
But it will not get power from a pen in my hand

PROLOGUE
to "Glimpses of Hell"

This book was extremely difficult for me to write. I had to recall traumas from my childhood that I had spent decades suppressing. I also had to recall stories and memories shared with me by well-meaning family and friends, their own bits and pieces of the whole abusive saga.

When I started to reluctantly recall the heartbreaking abuse and neglect of my childhood, the flood gates were opened. The traumatic events were, again, part of my every thought. They, and their evil influence, affected my present-day happiness throughout this writing process.

These stories and events were not necessarily known by friends and/or family. This is a book of deep dark secrets. The very idea of upsetting people that I care about while sharing this book made me consider not writing it at all.

This is my own perception of the trauma in my childhood, as I recollect it from my tainted memory. This is how the abuse affected me. If anyone is hurt or upset by the retelling or writing of this book, that is not my intention, and I am sorry. Despite how others may feel or think, I feel constrained to share me with you.

SYNOPSIS

My first book, "Snippets of Heaven," was a joyful retelling of stories on my grandparents' farm. We were loved, protected and encouraged by our grandparents and their faithful teachings of God.

When I was a child under the "care" of my parents, my sister and I were terribly abused. In my second book "Glimpses of Hell" I recall that terrible and heartbreaking childhood abuse.

Our parents had issues—mother was schizophrenic, our father alcoholic. They divorced when I was seven. Sis and I escaped the abuse . . . or did we? These stories are a part of who and why we are . . .

"It was dark and silent in the closet. How sad that I was okay with dark and silent. It was a reprieve from what it could be. Oh no . . . I heard something, footsteps. There was the sound of a light switch being flicked on.

"Light streamed under the door and through the key-hole. Someone was turning the handle on the closet door. The sound woke my little sister and she immediately started to cry. . . . I wish I could protect my little sister, but I am just one year older."

Melbalene

Melbalene was born in West Virginia in 1927. She was the third of twelve children. Her parents were good people. They were hard-working Baptist folk of "sturdy stock." Her father and her mother, both of Irish descent, were devoted to each other from a very young age.

Melbalene started life with her family in a small mining community in Bergoo, West Virginia. Melbalene loved this little community. The families were friends, adults and children alike. It was a comfortable, happy and safe place to live.

One day young Melbalene, about seven years old, came home from school. She was alone in the house as she searched the kitchen to find something to eat. She found one of her mother's fabulous biscuits from breakfast. She was so excited, as this was a favorite snack.

Melbalene danced around the red hot, pot-bellied stove in the middle of the front room. She was happily singing and dancing while waiting for her mother to return. One of the ties from her little pink apron touched against the very hot stove and immediately caught fire.

Tragically, in an instant, the back of her dress went up in flames. She ran hysterically from the little house. She ran through the neighborhood screaming, as the flames burned through her pretty dress and through her young skin, engulfing her back in red flames and black smoke.

Neighbors ran after her, eventually pushing her into the snow to put out the flames. As her mother knelt beside her, she lay sobbing in the snow. Her horrified mother couldn't even scoop her up to console her as she would scream out in agony. Melbalene's back, arms and legs, were burnt through the skin to the muscle and even to the bone in places.

This was a heartbreaking incident that befell such a sweet little girl and would affect her and her family forever. Melbalene was transferred to a hospital for special care, with not much chance to live. She surprised everyone by surviving the horrific fire. She was in the hospital lying on her stomach for over a year.

During that year her family took turns staying with her at the hospital. Her parents, along with aunts and uncles, kept watch as nurses and doctors tried to save this precious life. Nurses would soak large white towels in saltwater and lay them across her back. After the towels were dry, they were quickly pulled off, bringing bits of dead skin and infected tissue with it. It was a torturous process. Screaming could often be heard from her room, but the young girl survived the trauma.

Eventually Melbalene returned to her loving family in the little mining community. The many friends in the community were of great help to Melbalene and the family after this terrible ordeal. Their love, support and encouragement had so much to do with Melbalene's mental and physical healing.

Some years later the family moved to a farm in the community of Hacker Valley near Webster Springs, West Virginia. The farm was located on hundreds of acres. Melbalene's parents were thrilled. This was a big wonderful move, a dream come true for her parents.

The farm had been in her father's family for generations. Melbalene was not enchanted by the farm. It was far from her friends and the community she loved. It was so isolated in the mountains of West Virginia. To make matters worse, Melbalene had to start at a different school away from her dear friends in Bergoo.

The young people at her new school tormented and teased Melbalene. Young people can be so cruel. When they saw the terrible scars that covered her back, her arms, and her legs they had so much ammunition for their cruel verbal torment. She tried to avoid her classmates, but of course she could not. The constant teasing was more difficult to deal with than the scars she had carried through the years.

The family quickly grew from three children to twelve as each year passed. With each year that passed Melbalene became more determined to finish school and to move away from the farm. Melbalene grew into a beautiful young woman. People who knew the family would comment "there's not a plain kid in the bunch."

Melbalene was not only beautiful, she was a sweet and kind person as well. Years later comments were made that her facial features were a cross between actresses Sophia Loren and Liz Taylor, popular at that time. Unfortunately, so many people didn't see her natural beauty or notice her sweet personality. Some people saw only her terribly scarred body.

Despite her beauty, young Melbalene had a dark and deep-rooted problem, a hold-over from the trauma that had scarred her young body and haunted her dreams. Melbalene had "nervous breakdowns" or "mental episodes." Years later she was officially diagnosed with paranoid schizophrenia. Her mental illness became more severe as the years went by.

She was a young girl of fourteen, the first of many times her parents had her hospitalized. They were at a loss to control the violent and aggressive behavior that they did not understand. They had to protect their other children. It was difficult for her parents and siblings that she began manifesting these strange mental issues.

Ordinarily she was a sweet and caring individual. She was fun to be with and easy to talk to. She loved her family and friends. She would have episodes most often when she stopped taking her medications or if she was trying to deal with problems in her life that were just more than the medications could calm.

The horrific fire that burned and forever scarred this sweet little girl, affected her for her entire life. Through no fault of her own this mental illness and instability became a permanent part of her life and affected everyone she knew and loved.

Eventually some of her siblings began to believe that these angry, explosive episodes she was going through were a ploy to get attention. The turning of her siblings against her in this unfortunate way was just one more reason Melbalene couldn't wait to leave the farm.

Her emotional pain and trauma were very real. Her parents hospitalizing her, and her siblings' distrust, just caused the episodes to happen more frequently. It was such a sad and sorry cycle.

Melbalene was in and out of hospitals throughout her life. She was on and off medications regularly, usually at her own whim. It was a life of extreme highs and lows. At times, it was hell on earth for her and those closest to her.

Despite her mental and emotional challenges Melbalene found her first love at the young age of fifteen. She had wanted to get away from her family's farm from the moment they moved to it. There was a day when she and her mother had a terrible fight that prompted her to leave the farm.

The day after this terrible fight, Melbalene ran away from home. Her intentions were to stay with her grandma. As she traveled to

Grandma's home she went through the town of Webster Springs. At some point in her travel through town, she heard music. She was so excited about the music, she immediately set out to locate its source. Her trip to her grandmother's was postponed for a short time while she went on this adventure.

Melbalene followed the sound of the music to a tavern in town. She opened the door nervously and peeked inside. The inside was thick with smoke from cigarettes. The place was full of people clapping, dancing and singing to the music. She snuck through the door and went to the back of the tavern. She was mesmerized by the entire scene.

There was a band in the tavern, six young men playing guitars, harmonicas and one of them singing. She could not take her eyes off the singer. This was no farm boy. He was tall, handsome, laughing and singing. He was dressed so nice and neat her grandma would have said he was a true "dandy," a well-dressed man.

Melbalene was so focused on him, it was as if the smoke had parted just for her to see him better. She felt so strange, like nothing she had ever felt before. He was fabulous and just to look at him took her breath away. She didn't stay long. She left the tavern and headed to her grandma's.

She couldn't stop thinking of the young man in the band. Melbalene had always shared her every thought and feeling with her dear Grandma, but this particular time she did not tell her grandma anything, not one thought or feeling about the young singer in the tavern. However, he stayed in her thoughts, daily.

After a couple days with her grandma, Melbalene returned to her family at the farm. She promised her mother to never run away again but the very next year she started high school. She had an opportunity to leave the farm without running away.

Her grandma lived much closer to the high school in Webster Springs. Melbalene spoke with her, and with Grandmas' permission asked her parents if she could please stay with her grandma. The home was only walking distance to the high school.

Her parents reluctantly agreed, most especially since Melbalene would be helpful to her grandma who could certainly use some help as she was getting on in age. The arrangement would work out nicely for both Melbalene and her grandma.

Melbalene worked hard to do well in high school. She liked her classmates. She also did everything she could to help her grandma. Her grandma loved having Melbalene stay with her and would often say, "Child, you are spoiling me."

When Melbalene asked to go to town for a short while, her grandma was always pleased to give her permission. She told friends, "That child works so hard, she deserves a break." There were times the two of them went to town together.

But often, Melbalene would go alone. It was so easy for her to find reasons to go into town since her grandma lived so near Webster Springs. Sometimes she ran errands. On other occasions she went to the library or visited friends. Mostly, she snuck back to the tavern to watch the young singer she could not stop thinking of.

George

George was born in 1920 in West Virginia, the first of twelve children in his family. Both of his parents had immigrated from Germany, their birthplace. His parents were extremely strict. They were both born into Roman Catholic families but neither practiced their faith after they made their home in the USA.

George was devoted to his family but did not get along with his father, ever. They had a mutual dislike for each other as far back as George could recall. At the age of sixteen George left home and started working at a large hotel in Webster Springs. He quickly learned plumbing and electrical work from a long-time maintenance man at the hotel.

He tried to send money to his family, but his father refused to accept it. George never could recall when and why this mutual dislike started. He saw his siblings often usually in town, and he enjoyed it; but he didn't see his parents for many years, as his father forbade him to come to their home.

George worked at the hotel for five years. The hotel managers and owners were very pleased with him. He was extremely intelligent and learned quickly. When the United States joined in the fight during World War II, George joined the army. His employers at the hotel were sad to lose him to the army. He was in Europe from 1941 through 1945.

George liked the army. He liked the discipline and the structure. He learned anything he needed to know quickly. He went into combat and learned things he wished he'd never learned and saw things he wished he'd never seen. He did not like taking lives and was traumatized when young men he cared about were killed right in front of him.

George kept a kind of diary during his fighting years overseas for WWII. He started writing little notes on a dollar bill he happened to have with him. As time went on, he had stitched three other bills of currency from three other countries (Germany, Czechoslovakia and France) together to continue his diary. That little "diary" came to mean a lot to George during those years at war.

George and his combat buddies took up a couple bad habits to deal with the trauma of combat. They enjoyed cigarettes that were supplied by the army. Some of them, including George, also began to drink liquor, lots of liquor.

George never drank any type of alcohol or liquor before he joined up. In truth, it was dealing with the stress of combat that began his alcoholic escape. Very soon the alcohol was controlling George. Sadly, only the drinking could relieve the stress of combat.

George had every intention of re-enlisting in the army when his tour was up. He experienced a near miss in France when a dear friend stepped on a land mine and was killed. George suffered a concussion and some minor wounds, but the deepest wound, an emotional wound, was seeing his friend killed.

After spending three weeks in a hospital, George was sent back to France to take up the fight with his comrades in arms. He was not so fortunate this time, as within weeks of returning to his squad in France, he himself stepped on a land mine.

This time the entire inside of his left leg was blown apart. He spent several painful weeks in the same hospital in France. This stay included several surgeries to save his leg. The surgeons did save his leg, but he could not return to combat. His plans to reenlist in the army were as shattered as his leg.

George was transported back to the states. After several more weeks in the hospital in Charleston, West Virginia he was sent home. He left the hospital in Charleston with physical and emotional scars, a noticeable limp and one missing testicle—a stark reminder of the explosion he had survived. That last part upset him the most as doctors told him he may not be able to father children.

His mother overruled his father in this case, and George returned to his family's farm. He worked hard on the farm, although still struggling to completely heal from his physical and emotional wounds. For whatever reason, his father still had nothing to do with him.

Despite how he was treated by his father, George was determined to do well. Maybe he would even win his father's approval. He also found the time to take some classes in town and was soon a licensed electrician and plumber. He even took up a hobby to fill his occasional spare time. He taught himself to play the harmonica and then the guitar.

George always was a fast learner. He kept very busy trying to block the heartbreaking war memories from his mind. He still smoked cigarettes, pretty much non-stop, something he picked up in Europe. He also continued to drink, heavily.

It was the drinking that helped him forget and cope with wartime nightmares and daytime war visions. The liquor helped more than anything else he may have tried. Unfortunately, it was also the drinking that prompted his father to tell him, again, to leave the family farm. Despite his mother's frantic objections and genuine concern for her son, George left.

The hotel where George had worked prior to enlisting in the military was thrilled when he was forced to leave the farm. They hired him back immediately. George insisted they pay him more as he was now a licensed electrician and plumber. The hotel owners and managers went along with his request for more pay.

George was soon working full time at the hotel and had a small room there at no charge. He no longer tried to send money to his family, as it would have been to no avail. George had extra money and visited his favorite tavern almost every evening.

At that favorite tavern one evening, George met five young men who had recently returned from their tours of active duty overseas. The group of men and George hit it off immediately. They had not been as lucky as George to find jobs, so they started a band.

They explained that they were looking for one more man to join the band. They were hoping for someone that could play the guitar and maybe sing. Just for fun, and after a few drinks, George approached the group and claimed he could do both. George went on to say, as a bonus he could even play the harmonica.

To everyone's surprise, and especially George's, they believed he did all those things quite well. His hobby became a second job and best of all, he got his drinks for free wherever the band played. George was very happy about these exciting changes in his life.

George was doing well in his post-war life. He was doing better than many of the young men that had returned home after he did. Even the men in his band were struggling. The band was all they had. George, on the other hand, had a full-time job through the week and played in the band on weekends.

George had something else his friends in the band did not have, but this was not a good thing. He was haunted by memories of the war. George drank more than his band members. Drinking helped him get past the nightmares. Many nights his buddies would literally carry him back to his room.

Their compassion for George had no bounds. They had fought in the war also but had not been through as much as George, and this affected him deeply. None of his friends in the band suffered nightmares that kept them awake or daytime visions that haunted them. Perhaps it was his drinking that made his memories worse.

But band members were always there for him without question.

George liked his day job and was good at it. George loved the band and was a great singer and guitarist. George even invested in a steel guitar and found his passion in that instrument. Many people had never seen or heard of such a thing, not even his band members.

This guitar was a squared off steel instrument that sat on a table. It had a completely different sound than the regular guitars that were used in the band. Suddenly, with the addition of this new instrument, their band was in demand. George had a true passion and talent for his steel guitar, and it showed in his music.

George settled into this new life and was very happy. When friends or family mentioned their concern for his heavy drinking, he did not acknowledge a problem. It certainly was not a problem for him.

Regularly, his band buddies carried him home from the bar. At his job at the hotel, the older men he worked with were often put in a position to cover for George. George's drinking would interfere with his ability to do the job that he loved, but he didn't seem to notice.

What he did notice was that he got a lot of attention wherever the band went, as did the other band members. George laughed at the attention and just kept busy with his life. Then something happened, something unexpected. There was this girl. This beautiful, quiet, shy and mysterious girl.

George first noticed her in the back of the bar they played in when they were in Webster Springs. This bar was their home base. She was very young, and George thought that she was the most beautiful girl he had ever seen. This was quite something coming from a young man who had met beautiful women in France and Germany during the war.

She had long, dark wavy hair and was dressed so modestly. She glanced in his direction and would quickly look away. He noticed her full pouty lips. Was she wearing red lipstick or were they just that red? He noticed she wore rather fancy little boots that were out of place with her plain modest outfit.

The band made its regular rounds of several bars and taverns in nearby towns. The turnout was always great wherever they played.

George suddenly didn't seem to notice the wonderful turnouts. He was often preoccupied with thoughts elsewhere, anticipating their return to Webster.

All the band members enjoyed returning to play at their home base in Webster Springs more than anyplace else. Especially George—upon every return to home base he'd look for the shy beauty, always alone, in the back of the bar.

There were several months during which he didn't see her. He didn't even know her name. And then, mysteriously, there she was. Although it had been months, as soon as he saw her, he had the same strong and strange feelings.

Now whenever he saw her, he couldn't breathe. You can't sing if you can't breathe. Then George couldn't think, you can't play guitar if you can't think. What a spell she cast on him. The young beauty with the fancy little boots.

His band mates figured out quickly what was ailing George. They teased him mercilessly. George, who never really paid much attention to all the ladies that loved the band, could not take his eyes off this young beauty. He didn't even know her name. He and his band mates started referring to her as "Boots" (a nickname she would keep forever).

One evening, as George relaxed with his friends during a short break for the band, he saw the girl sneak in. It was quiet compared to the noise when they were playing. He saw her proceed to her usual spot far in the back along the wall. Suddenly the door into the bar opened.

He did not see who had opened the door, but he distinctly heard a woman's voice yell out "Melbalene Marie." The young girl immediately left the bar. Melbalene was her name, Melbalene Marie. It seemed like such an exotic name and she was, without a doubt, his new passion. Melbalene, with the fancy little boots.

Moonlight Meadow

Melbalene's grandma loved having her granddaughter stay with her. She was a sweet girl and was so helpful. Her granddaughter worked hard every day. She was doing well in high school and had made many friends. Melbalene liked the short walk to school from her grandma's home.

Whatever needed to be done, Melbalene helped without attitude or incident. Of Melbalene's many friends at high school, her grandma knew most of them. Sometimes her friends would walk with Melbalene to Grandma's after school and have fresh milk and warm cookies.

On other occasions Melbalene would stop at the library after school and study with her friends. The living arrangement between Melbalene and her grandma continued to be very good for them both. Even Melbalenes' parents were pleased how everything had turned out.

There were times Melbalene would walk to town to do some shopping for her grandma. Occasionally grandma and Melbalene would walk to town together. Shopping together did not happen often, as grandma would quickly become tired—sometimes so much so, that friends would drive them back to the house.

One day Melbalene set out to town to do some shopping. No sooner had she left the house than Grandma recalled something else she needed. She stepped outside onto the porch and called after Melbalene but could not be heard.

Grandma snatched up her purse and followed her granddaughter into town. It was a beautiful day and the walk would do her good. Plus, she would catch up with Melbalene soon enough.

She could see Melbalene in the distance very clearly. She called a couple more times but Melbalene did not turn around. Suddenly Melbalene did something very strange. Grandma did not expect to see her sweet dear granddaughter turn into a tavern. A tavern! If she hadn't seen this herself, she would have never believed it.

Young ladies don't go into taverns, and they certainly don't go in alone. They don't go into taverns when they've told their grandma that they were going to town to do some shopping for the woman they loved. Melbalene's grandmother was very upset, something that did not often happen.

Grandma knew exactly and immediately what she was to do. Grandma was going into that tavern to retrieve her wayward granddaughter. When she got to the entrance of the bar, she quietly opened the door to peek in. She saw Melbalene standing against the back wall. Sweet and gentle grandma angrily called her name and Melbalene quickly left the tavern.

As soon as she stepped outside with her dear grandmother, Melbalene began to cry. The look on her grandma's face broke her heart. She knew she had been deceitful and dishonest, so unlike her. Tears welled up in the old woman's eyes also.

"I'm sorry, Grandma, I'm so sorry," Melbalene tried to apologize through her tears. "I didn't know how to explain so I just never told you. I only stood at the back against the wall, nothing else, ever." With teary eyes grandma asked, "Whatever possessed you to do such a thing?"

Melbalene told her grandmother the whole story of the day she ran away from her home on the farm and heard the music as she walked through town. She explained the feeling she had for the singer in the band and that she was lost and confused. These feelings were so strange and new to her.

It just so happened that grandma, who was a young girl once herself, knew exactly what Melbalene was trying to explain. She marched her granddaughter right back into that tavern. The young men in the band were still sitting around the table on a break.

George looked up to see a silver-haired woman standing by the table. "Young man, do you have feelings for my granddaughter?" The tiny, angry lady stepped aside and there stood Melbalene, right there next to him. He just stared, not breathing, not thinking. It finally occurred to him that he must look like a complete idiot. He heard someone say "Yes ma'am," in his own shaky voice.

Melbalene's grandmother just kept on, to the girl's complete and total shock and embarrassment. She stood next to her grandma through the entire speech. She could not take her eyes off the young man. Melbalene was suddenly dizzy as he glanced her way.

"She will not spend time with you in this bar."

"Yes ma'am," George replied as he finally stood up.

Melbalene thought, "He's so tall." She felt weak. Next to him her grandma looked even tinier, standing there in front of him shaking a finger right in his face. "What is your name, young man?" Grandma demanded.

"My name is George, ma'am," he replied meekly.

"Well, George, you will court her like a proper young man should."

"Yes ma'am," George replied, still not breathing. His band buddies around the table were trying not to laugh. They were just as tickled with this tiny silver-haired lady as they were with their friend's discomfort.

Grandma gave her name and address to the tall handsome singer. She took Melbalene by the hand and marched her out of the tavern. As soon as they left the bar, his buddies burst out laughing. They had enjoyed this entertainment immensely.

George stood there for the longest time, in a daze, staring at the door where they had disappeared. What had just happened? He could hear his friends' laughter; they sounded so far away. Then a thought came to him, his life was about to change drastically.

The courtship lasted over two years. George was the "proper young man" through the whole thing. He didn't even realize that wartime memories and nightmares did not often come to him and his drinking had cut way back. His every spare thought was of Melbalene.

When he met her family, he liked them. The parents and her siblings were kind to him. They were welcoming and openly affectionate with each other. This was nothing like his cold and strict family. His feelings for Melbalene grew even stronger.

Over those couple years of courting George worked faithfully at his day job at the hotel, but he slowly pulled away from the band. George was seven years older than Melbalene. A short time after she finished high school, the couple were married at the Baptist church. Her entire family attended; his family did not.

George never noticed the scars on his beautiful young wife. She was so much more than those scars. Melbalene didn't care that her husband was injured in the war to the point that he maybe could not father children with her. She was very happy with her husband and her life.

They found a small apartment in town. Though George had bought a small car after they were married, he walked to work at the hotel most days. Melbalene didn't drive but could easily walk to town to do errands or visit friends. They both saw their siblings often and Melbalene lived close enough to her grandma that she still helped every week.

On occasion they would drive to the farm to visit her parents. Melbalene enjoyed the visits, since she no longer lived on the farm. George's parents still had nothing to do with their son even after he married. He knew this was due to his father's heartless and foolish insistence.

The young couple were soon expecting their first child. They were so excited. George, of course, was particularly thankful, as he would be a father after all, despite his war injury. Their life was good. Melbalene thrived emotionally and George had stopped drinking entirely. He didn't even think about it.

Then the young couple suffered a terrible blow; without warning, the hotel closed. This was such an unexpected shock. George was suddenly without a job. His band friends (all of whom were single) still had their band and offered to take him on, but that would not be enough to care for his little family.

They had to give up their apartment, which they both liked so much. Melbalene stayed with her grandma while George looked for work in the nearby town of Charlestown. George thought, and rightly so, since Charleston was a much bigger town, he had a better chance of finding a job.

George found a job rather quickly. The company that hired him was impressed with his work history and the fact that he had fought for his country. They were looking for someone to add to their service crew of men that did electrical and plumbing. How perfect for George.

Melbalene joined George in Charleston. They found a house for rent and settled in. Melbalene was sad to be away from everything she loved. She missed her family, especially her grandma. She was not comfortable or happy in Charleston. George had to be gentle as she became more unstable. He was taking an occasional drink to handle the stress of this new unexpected change in their lives.

Melbalene had to take a bus into town when she needed to shop. She was quite pregnant by now and the grocery bags were heavy for her. One day, after taking the bus to do some grocery shopping, a young man offered to help her carry the bags of groceries home. Grateful for his offer of help as she was so tired, she reluctantly accepted.

A couple weeks later, Melbalene again went to town to shop. She again met the young man on the bus while returning home. They conversed on the bus. He explained he was a photographer for a small newspaper in Charleston and took the bus back and forth to work.

Melbalene was fascinated. How wonderful to be able to make a living taking photos. She was also quite shocked when the young man asked if he could take a few photos of her. She laughed as she was large with child and could not understand why he would want to do such a thing.

He said they were doing a story about young couples starting out in Charleston. He then told her she was so very beautiful and would be a perfect photo subject. Melbalene was suddenly uncomfortable. She told the young man no photos, but she did allow him to help her carry those darned heavy grocery bags since he had offered.

When George came home later and they were sharing the events of their day, Melbalene was tickled to tell her husband about the young reporter who had wanted to take her photo as, to quote him "she was so beautiful." To her shock, George was very angry, and he began screaming at her. He was jealous, something she had never seen in him before. He had certainly never screamed at her.

He told her it was careless for her to associate with a stranger. It was not safe for either her or their unborn child. Melbalene was hurt—everyone around her was a stranger. Also, the conversation had been on a crowded bus and seemed perfectly safe. When she tried to kiss George to put an end to the fight, she could smell liquor on his breath before he turned away.

On another evening shortly after this encounter, George returned home from work to find the young photographer in front of the house taking photos. He came up to George and introduced himself, saying he wanted to take some photos of the couple for a story his newspaper was doing.

George was furious. He snatched the camera, threw it to the ground, breaking it into pieces and angrily chased the young photographer off with threats. He charged into the house and demanded, screaming, to know how this man knew where they lived.

Melbalene tearfully explained that he had recently carried groceries for her. She went on to say she had not told George this previously as she did not want to make him even more angry.

She had not even been aware that the photographer was outside the house that day. She leaned toward her husband hoping to calm him. As she came closer, she could smell the foul liquor heavy on his breath.

She turned away and ran up the stairs. George followed her, not yet done with some things he wanted to say to his young wife. Melbalene was heartbroken and as George came to the top of the stairs, she shouted hysterically, "Stay away from me, you've been drinking."

George struck her across the face with all the strength of his full angry, drunken force. Melbalene tumbled violently down the stairs. She lay unconscious at the bottom of the stairs where her baby died inside her from the terrible fall.

Melbalene later swore to anyone who dared ask that she had

stumbled. At the hospital she delivered the dead body of their son. The couple returned with his little body to Webster Springs to be with their families. This would become a dark turning point in their lives.

George's father approached his son—the first time they had communicated in years. He reminded his son of the beautiful meadow on the farm. He offered the meadow as the final place for the grandson he had never seen and would never know.

The meadow was beautiful, George remembered it well. What a sadly appropriate resting place for the baby that would have been Gerald. Offered by the father who had disowned him, to the son he would not speak to, for a grandson he would never know, George was too heartbroken to fight over the offer. He sadly agreed.

Their families, both families, were at the meadow the day the baby boy was buried. It was a solemn, quiet, heart-wrenching occasion. Everyone from both families would kiss the young couple as each of them slowly left the meadow. Soon the couple was alone in their sorrow, standing together in the meadow.

It was just the two of them. The shattered young husband and broken young wife. They stayed there, standing and staring at the tiny grave, while the sun set, and the moon rose, Melbalene's sanity was slowly slipping away. They both stayed for a very long time, staring at the tiny grave in the meadow in the moonlight.

Buckhannon

Melbalene believed in "until death do us part" even when her love for her husband died with her baby boy. The couple returned to Charleston. She was a good and dutiful wife to George in every respect. Their little house was always clean and neat. There was always a nice meal waiting when he returned home from work.

George worked long hours, which was fine. What was sad is that he came home very late, long after work was done. He always stopped for a few drinks, so the meal he came home to was almost always cold. The cold meals made him angry and he screamed, accusing Melbalene of being a bad wife.

The long hours alone and the constant screaming from her husband took a terrible toll on Melbalene. She was heartbroken over the loss of their child. She cried most every day. She was very thin and frail. She went through her days with wide teary eyes and shaky hands.

George finally took notice and insisted she visit the local doctor. There was no cure for the loss of a child or an angry husband. She was often emotional and hysterical. The doctor tried several medications to calm her.

Eventually the doctor suggested that Melbalene spend some time at the hospital. Perhaps more specialized physicians could better determine how best to help Melbalene. This was when she was first diagnosed with schizophrenia by the specialists. George had never heard of such a thing.

The day Melbalene was released from the hospital the physicians explained to the couple that she would have to take her medication faithfully. He also cautioned George that his wife should be carefully watched. They also informed the couple that Melbalene was expecting another child.

Melbalene and George wanted to be happy about this baby, but it brought the loss of their baby boy to the forefront of both their thoughts. George worked even harder but was not happy, so he also drank more. Melbalene was a good wife, but there was no joy, no love. She felt so alone, lost and depressed.

This was not the same happy couple that had thrived in Webster Springs. George didn't have his buddies to turn to or lean on and Melbalene missed her loving and supportive family. Their life together became a cycle of his drinking and screaming and her crying. His screaming often led to his slapping and hitting his wife, a new and sad development that occurred often if not daily.

George's heavy drinking was also affecting his job. There was no one to cover for him when his work failed. There was no one to carry him home when he drank too much at the bars after work. George eventually lost his job.

He did try to find another job, but he was not the same determined man. He was angry and out of sorts and people could see this when he spoke to anyone about working for them. To make matters worse, as time went by, Melbalene's health and her pregnancy were threatened. The couple had no choice. They returned to Webster Springs.

They stayed with Melbalene's grandma for a very short time. This short stay was a wonderful healing time for Melbalene with her grandma's love and care. George was on his best behavior and hid his drinking well. He most certainly did not scream at his wife or hit her with Grandma around.

Eventually Melbalene's parents came to visit with some good news. Melbalene had an uncle in Buckhannon, West Virginia. He lived in a big house near the city. He offered for the couple to stay with him and his family (as he had lots of room) while George looked for a job.

The couple was a little uncertain about the offer but had no choice. They were soon relocated to Buckhannon. As it turned out, Melbalene was pampered by her aunt and cousins and George really got along with the uncle. The young couple's health and outlook improved. Their relationship seemed on the mend.

George walked to Buckhannon every day, faithfully trying to find work. There was no money to buy gas for his car. Late fall turned to a frigid winter. Melbalene helped as much as she was permitted, although she was "heavy with child" and her aunt preferred to pamper her. The couple tried to earn their keep, helping around the house, since there was no money coming in.

Melbalene and George were quite happy and healthy at this point. They had been well cared for by Melbalene's family. George still had a drink on occasion, but there was no screaming or hitting directed at his wife. With the stress gone, Melbalene thrived.

Early one morning the family woke up to the winter wind howling and snow falling. George had already left the house to walk to town as his car was buried beneath the thickly fallen snow. He was supposed to speak with a friend that had a lead on a job. Melbalene and her aunt had made breakfast for everyone else. Suddenly there was a knock at the door.

A neighbor was at the door to say that the weather had taken a terrible turn. There was already over a foot of snow on the ground. The wind was so fierce and blowing so hard, you could barely stand outside, let alone see anything. Melbalene's uncle left the house with the neighbor. "I'll be right back," he said, "just want to check things out."

You could hear the screeching of the wind, the sound mounting with every minute. Snow continued to fall nonstop and heavy. You could feel the old house shaking from the forces of the wind against it. The power went out and the lights with it. Thank goodness, there was a nice fire roaring in the fireplace keeping the house warm and cozy.

The men returned shortly to announce that there was nothing moving on the roads, not a thing. In the distance they could both see that the town of Buckhannon was blacked out, as there was no power in town either. The uncle wondered where George was and hoped he was okay.

Both the uncle and his neighbor announced they were staying home. There was no need to venture to town with no power. Obviously, the factory where they both worked together could not run without it. The neighbor agreed. They would just hunker down and wait out the storm.

As it turned out, there was to be no hunkering down. Melbalene had waited to say anything, as she wanted to be sure. She was now very sure that she was in labor. The family could barely hear her announcement over the howling winds.

Neither man could get to his car. Both vehicles were buried under the snow just as George's had been. Even if they could move the cars, there was no traffic on the roads as those roads were also beneath the deep snow. Melbalene was frightened as her pains became more and more difficult to manage.

Her aunt suggested that she could help with the delivery right there in the house. Melbalene feared losing her baby without a doctor. She knew the hospital in Buckhannon was a couple miles walk away—a bit of a jaunt even in good weather. When her uncle, feeling quite helpless and concerned, finally said they could maybe walk. Melbalene quickly agreed to tackle the journey.

Her aunt was beyond worried about this plan, but she knew she could not change her niece's mind. If Melbalene stayed at the house and lost her baby, she would forever regret not attempting the walk. Ultimately, the decision was Melbalene's and she chose to walk. But where was her husband?

Everyone bundled up against the terrible weather. The men walked in front of Melbalene both shoveling a path and blocking the howling wind the best they could. She followed close behind with a young cousin on either side to help steady her. The boys were so concerned. They could not believe they were attempting this trek. They certainly could not imagine how Melbalene was so willing to do this.

    The trek was torture, and the cold wind numbed them right through their clothes and down to their bones. They could not see through the thick falling snow. The men could hardly hold onto the shovel handles as their fingers numbed. The young boys had a difficult time steadying their precious cousin. What kept them all moving forward was Melbalene's determination despite intense labor pains.

    It was truly amazing when they arrived at the hospital. Miraculous was the only explanation for arriving at a destination traveling blind. Each of them wondered how they had gotten safely to the hospital—they couldn't even see as they trudged through the drifts.

    Saint Joseph's Hospital was a Catholic hospital, yet none of them had ever seen a nun before. Nuns in their habits rushed to help them, each carrying a lantern. It was a rather eerie sight.

    They were all exhausted, especially pregnant Melbalene. She was in full hard labor by this time. She collapsed to the floor and was carried to a room by four of the nuns and laid on a bed. She was surrounded by nuns and doctors. Gazing around and seeing the nuns all dressed in black, she thought she had died and was definitely not in heaven.

The nuns showed the men to a different area of the hospital, where they were attended to. The nuns fussed over the four men to the point of embarrassment. These men were not accustomed to being cared for by strangers, and these women were not only strangers, they were just plain strange.

Melbalene was in the labor room in dire distress. At this point she was so weak. To make matters worse her baby was breach, meaning the baby was coming feet/butt first. As if the trek was not difficult enough, this labor was now also difficult, if not life-threatening for mother and baby alike. The only recourse for the doctors was to attempt to turn the baby inside her.

Melbalene was rather delirious from exhaustion and pain, which was probably a good thing at this point. She was unaware of just how many times the doctors tried to reposition the unborn baby inside her. Eventually the determined baby was finally birthed in a breach position. Against all odds, and to the thrill of nuns and doctors alike, Brenda was born screaming very loudly and looking very healthy.

The men recovering in another area of the hospital heard the very loud screaming of the newborn. A nun ran joyfully into the room to announce that mother and baby girl were doing very well despite the ordeal they had been through. The four men were happier and warmer but still silent in shock. They suddenly wondered, where was George?

The men wanted to see Melbalene and her newborn daughter, but the nuns discouraged it. Melbalene was exhausted and would probably sleep for hours. The nuns were keeping a close protective watch over baby Brenda, and Melbalene to be sure all was good with both mother and baby.

The men decided to return home and hopefully locate George. He should be here with his wife and child. The four set out, the snow was just as deep but at least the wind had eased up. They found the path they had shoveled and could now see where they were heading. The three-mile return trip was so much easier, especially now that Melbalene was safely at the hospital with her newborn daughter.

When the men made it back to the house, they were now able to laugh about their wild wintry adventure. They were again very cold, but they were not scared or stressed over concern for Melbalene. There was now joy over this great joint accomplishment and the new baby girl in the family.

The uncle hugged his neighbor enthusiastically and said they could not have done this without him. He was a good neighbor. As the uncle and his sons walked into the house, the look on the aunt's face immediately dampened their joyful celebration.

She pointed to the floor in front of the fireplace. There lay George. They were concerned at the sight, and then the aunt explained. "I don't know what possessed the man. He is completely and positively drunk. He stumbled into the house and has been passed out right there by the fireplace ever since."

George had been somewhere drinking this whole time. Had he ever been looking for a job when he went to town every day? He was too drunk to inquire about his pregnant wife or even make any attempt to cover up his drunken condition before returning to the house.

As the uncle stood staring at the drunk unconscious man on the floor, he said aloud, "Where did he get the money for all this drinking?"

With a puzzled and concerned look on his face, the uncle went to a drawer in the kitchen. There was a box in the drawer where the uncle always put a good amount of cash every payday. The box had been full of cash. He opened the box and his face went white. There were now only a couple of bills left in the box. The entire stash was missing. He and his family were in shock. They all looked toward the man on the kitchen floor. How could he have done such a thing? They had no doubt; he was the thief.

They had opened their home and their hearts to this man. They were shocked and heartbroken over this sad turn of events, yet they felt worse for Melbalene and her newborn daughter.

Melbalene's uncle and aunt did not know what to do about this dilemma. They could not go on as if nothing had happened. Stealing from the family was a big deal. They considered calling the police and probably should have. Then again, they were compelled above all else to do whatever was necessary to help and protect Melbalene.

It was decided that they would discuss this with the couple when Melbalene returned to their home from the hospital. They would let Melbalene make the decision on what she wanted to do. They now had to figure just what they would say to the niece they loved. How could they possibly explain what her drunken husband had done to her family without breaking her heart?

Remembrance

(written by Melbalene - Dec 14, 1950)

It was 1950, the month of November,
The day that ones involved remember,
We awoke one cold and snowy morn,
To find ourselves in the midst of a storm.
My cousins and uncle shoveled a path in the snow,
Because thru this storm we were sure I would go.
My child was due most anytime,
A way through the storm we would have to find.
But with God's help we trudged on thru the storm,
At the beginning of dawn our Brenda was born,
I thank God every day for her presence so dear,
I pray he will always keep us near.
We count our blessings but still feel sad,
Because she will always miss her Dad.
"Tell me why my Daddy won't come Home"

Sewickley Valley

Melbalene and her baby girl, Brenda, stayed at Saint Joseph's Hospital for over a week. They were very well cared for by the nuns whom Melbalene found to be very strange. But she came to love every nun that took care of her and her baby daughter. Both mother and baby were doing wonderfully, stronger with every passing day.

During the days that Melbalene stayed at the hospital with her baby, the terrible storm grew worse as the week progressed. It broke all records up to that time and was soon called "the Great Appalachian Storm of 1950." It was labeled a winter cyclone. Snow fell up to 65 inches deep. Record breaking temperatures plunged to 10 degrees below zero and felt much colder with winds that exceeded 150 miles per hour.

After the power was restored the snow continued to pile up and the roads remained impassable. Her family and her husband called every day but were not able to travel to the hospital to visit. The vehicles and roads were buried beneath the snow. Finally, Melbalene and her baby were able to return to her loving family and her husband.

The nuns were so excited. Those determined and persistent ladies had compelled the driver of a county snowplow to please drive Melbalene and her baby to her uncle's farm to be with her husband. Praise God. The snowplow was the only vehicle large and powerful enough to drive through the record-breaking snow drifts.

Melbalene was jubilant with the healthy baby in her arms as she walked into the house, but the mood in the house was somber. Her aunt and uncle both hugged her, then, practically in unison said, "We have to talk with you."

George was sitting at the kitchen table and had not even stood up to greet his wife and new baby girl. It had been a full week, and he made no attempt to greet them. Melbalene was so hurt, but things quickly got worse. He had his face hidden in both his hands and did not even look up. Her aunt and uncle started talking. Everything went fuzzy real fast.

She could hear her family speaking, they sounded far away. She heard every word quite plainly, every sad, heartbreaking word. They explained about her drunken husband passed out on the floor. They explained about the stolen money, and that they had not called the police. Her husband would have been sent to jail, and what good would that have done anyone?

Tears ran down Melbalene's face. She was beyond horrified at what her husband had done. Her aunt held her hand, tears streaming down her face also. They talked about his drinking and if he ever had tried to find a job. George said nothing, with his head still down and his face hidden. His actions and his silence seemed to answer that question.

They kept talking—every word more painful than the last. It was so uncomfortable in the room, and in her heart. Melbalene's hard labor had been easier for her to deal with, it was a natural pain. But this, the emotional hurt and humiliation, was more then she could bear. She felt herself mentally slipping away, slowly escaping into insanity.

Her uncle apologized for having to tell her any of this. He also said he had a plan and wanted to hear her response. He did not even mention his concern over George's thoughts on the plan. The uncle did not care what George thought. It was against his wishes that George was even still in his home. If not for his own loving wife's insistence, he would have thrown drunken George out into the snow that first night.

The uncle explained that a friend had shared with him that a coal mining company was opening a new mine in Sewickley Valley, Pennsylvania. Her uncle's friend said he could get George a job there. George did not want to work in a coal mine, but he said nothing as he had no choice in the matter.

The problem with the plan was that the mine would not open for a couple months. Her uncle went on to say that he could use help at their home (as it was also a small farm) for those couple of months until the mining company was up and running. George could help the family on the farm, without pay, for the next two months to help pay back what had been stolen. Melbalene slowly started to walk away.

Her aunt asked, "Melbalene dear, what do you think?" Melbalene answered, "That is just fine, auntie, I am so very sorry about the stolen money." She quietly left for her room with her baby daughter clutched tight in her arms. She was humiliated and broken. She did not even look at George as she walked away. There was such a feeling of loss that washed over her.

Later, after she had rested, her aunt spoke with her. Her aunt explained that the next couple of months would be a good time for Melbalene to do some thinking. Did she even want to follow her husband to Sewickley Valley? She was more than welcome to stay here with her precious baby. The family had plenty of room and they so loved having her.

Or perhaps, her aunt went on, you could return to your family farm in Webster Springs for a while. Give your husband time to settle in Sewickley Valley. Both women knew how much her own mother would love to spend time with her daughter and baby granddaughter.

Melbalene appreciated her aunt's genuine love and concern. She also knew, as much as her uncle would prefer not to deal with George, he would do anything to help his dear niece. It was just too much to deal with. Despite the knowledge of her family's love, Melbalene soon fell into an unhealthy frame of mind and a dangerous emotional state.

She was not herself and was not even aware that her baby needed care. Was she her other self? She spoke of things that made no sense. She recalled things happening to her in the house that her aunt and uncle knew for a fact had never happened. They were at a loss and their genuine love could not fix this.

The family had known about Melbalene's past history of emotional breakdowns prior to her stay with them, but they had never witnessed this firsthand. They had never seen anyone go through such a dramatic change. Melbalene was completely out of touch with the world around her.

They could hardly recognize the woman that Melbalene became during this emotional breakdown. She was so angry, striking out verbally and physically. It was frightening. Her aunt and uncle both agreed with George when he suggested that his wife should spend some time at the hospital. Hopefully, the doctors could find a way to calm and stabilize her. She would probably need to have a change in her medications.

Although she had taken medications faithfully since coming to stay with her aunt and uncle, the added stress was more than the medications could handle. When baby Brenda was just a month old, she was left in the care of Melbalene's family. Melbalene had to spend time at the same hospital they had recently left. The nuns were so sweet and gentle with the broken young mother.

Melbalene was at the hospital for almost three weeks. In that time, George truly did work hard to repay the family. It was not a comfortable arrangement—still, it was much better than being sent to jail, which he knew was the alternative as the uncle reminded him often.

When Melbalene was able to return to the family, her baby and George, she was so quiet and withdrawn. She had some problems remembering anything that had happened prior to her hospital stay. She knew the baby was hers, only because the family told her so. This was beyond sad.

In a couple of weeks George would be taking his wife and baby daughter to Sewickley Valley in Pennsylvania. Under the loving care of her aunt, Melbalene was soon much improved. Her aunt took her aside and explained that her offer still stood. Melbalene could stay with them and let George get settled in Sewickley Valley.

The aunt again explained that Melbalene might prefer to return to her family in Webster Springs for a while. She would be loved and cared for wherever she chose to go, (except maybe with her husband) at least for a while. Her aunt went so far as to voice her concerns about George's drinking. The choice was ultimately Melbalene's.

Melbalene said, "I no longer have a choice. I'm pregnant." Her aunt was shocked. She had not expected for her to be pregnant so quickly. Melbalene went on to say she had to make things work with her husband. She could not burden either family with herself as well as her two babies.

And besides, Melbalene went on, George had not been drinking any liquor these past two months. That statement did not make her aunt feel any better. In fact, it caused a deep feeling of foreboding. The truth was, her aunt was not all that sure that George had not found a way to continue drinking. She did not trust her niece's husband at all.

Very shortly after this conversation, a few days perhaps, arrangements were made for the very helpful neighbor to drive the family to Sewickley Valley. This would be the chance for their new start in a life together. Her aunt, being the woman in the bunch, could not shake the feeling of foreboding. She prayed she was just being over-sensitive and that her niece would be just fine.

It was a difficult and tearful goodbye for Melbalene and her family. Her aunt and uncle were teary-eyed. Her big, strapping cousins, who made her feel so safe, were beside themselves with sadness. They had come to love little Brenda as one of their own. Oh, how they would miss Melbalene and her baby girl.

It was a three-hour drive to Sewickley Valley, which was about 140 miles from Buckhannon. It was an uncomfortable and silent drive. Her uncle's neighbor knew about the theft at his friends' home and had nothing to say to George. He was doing his friend a favor.

He was more than happy to get George far from his friends. He was very concerned for Melbalene and her baby. He had been married for over forty years and would have never done the things George did. He would certainly have not humiliated his wife. In his opinion, there was something very wrong with George. He did not trust the man and with good reason.

The neighbor dropped them off at Sewickley Valley Mining Company and the couple checked in at the mining company office. The man in the office said they'd been expecting them and he would show them the housing area. Each family was given a small house to live in if they worked for the company. He went on to explain there was a small fee for the house, but it was so much less than renting outside the company.

The little family was taken to the house. All they had with them was their clothes. It was a tiny house, just one bedroom. Melbalene knew she could make it work for them. There might be room for their baby daughter with them in their own bedroom.

She was a little disappointed but did not tell George, as he was already against this idea. Her family had lived in a coal mining home for years and she recalled that it was so much nicer and larger than this tiny house. Eventually, God willing, there would be two babies. This tiny house was going to get very crowded very quickly.

They settled in. George had to start work first thing the very next day. The company was shorthanded, as they just opened the mining operation. They were doing what they could with the men they had, probably by overworking them.

The next morning George left early for his first day working in the mine. Melbalene walked to the company store for some groceries, with a small amount of cash her aunt had given her. The store was not far but she had to carry her baby there and back and she was pregnant.

After she found the couple things she needed, she pulled out her cash to pay for the groceries. The groceries were expensive at the company store. The lady at the counter explained that they took no cash as the grocery amount would come off her husband's pay along with the rent.

Melbalene returned to the house to make a meal. She was exhausted. She was pregnant and had carried her groceries and baby girl home. She was missing her aunt and uncle. She was missing her family on the farm. She was even missing the man she had married.

What had happened to the happy, talented man who had stolen her heart. She felt very lost and alone. She was relieved that her aunt and uncle had helped them instead of calling the police after the theft. But this "new life together" was going to be more difficult than she had imagined.

When George came home that evening, he was angry. He didn't like this work he was forced to do. He was no longer grateful for the chance the uncle had given him. The couple ate Melbalene's nice meal in silence that night and many others.

Life went on day to day. Neither of the young people were happy with their situation or each other. Despite their problems, each of them did get to know some people. George made a couple friends at work and Melbalene enjoyed her neighbors.

Eventually, the men at work invited George to stop and have a couple drinks with them. When he came home late that evening, he was very drunk. He was more angry than usual over the fact that his dinner was cold.

He screamed at his wife. The baby cried and Melbalene was terrified, tears filling her eyes and fear filling her heart. She had lost one baby to his anger. She would have to be very careful.

Matters got even worse when George picked up his first paycheck. The pay came to next to nothing. George had worked so hard at the job he hated, but by the time the company had deducted the rent, groceries and George's bar tab from his check, there was not much left.

Over the next few months, George went from screaming to screaming and hitting. Every night was the same sad scene. The neighbors could hear as the homes were so close. Melbalene never said anything, but her new friends were concerned for her. Not only did they hear what was happening, she was starting to act very strange, and why not?

It was inevitable; Melbalene fell completely apart emotionally. George was called to the office one day at work and told there was a problem at home. When he got to the house, a couple neighbor ladies were outside with baby Brenda. George could hear Melbalene yelling the strangest things from inside the house. There was also a lot of profanity, words Melbalene never used.

From inside the tiny house they could hear Melbalenes loud screams about her power from God and ranting about the things He wanted her to do. The hysterical voice was most definitely Melbalene's, but the things she was screaming sent shivers and fear through her neighbors and her husband.

George and the neighbors could hear the violent sounds of things being thrown and things being broken. Suddenly Melbalene was standing at the front window. She started screaming obscenities and pounding violently against the glass with her fists. The glass window shattered. Glass was flying in every direction. Melbalene was standing in the window sobbing, with blood streaming from the cuts on her hands and arms.

It was a frightening experience for everyone. It was heartbreaking and unsettling to see what Melbalene was capable of. What had possessed her to do such a thing? She had caused harm to herself. She could have hurt her baby daughter and the ladies standing shocked in the front yard. George made immediate arrangements to take his pregnant wife to the hospital.

When George returned to the house, he was alone. He was compelled to explain to the neighbors his wife's fragile emotional condition and history of mental breakdowns. Fortunately, the neighbor ladies offered to care for Brenda until his wife was able to return home from her hospital stay.

After several weeks Melbalene returned to the tiny house. The neighbor ladies who had cared for baby Brenda in her absence noticed how withdrawn and emotionless Melbalene acted upon her return. She was not the same person. Perhaps it was the medications. (They did not know she had undergone electric shock therapy, a very common practice at that time.) She didn't seem to know anyone. It took several weeks before she was more herself.

The ladies really liked Melbalene; she was a sweet person. They found her situation so sad but also very frightening. Melbalene had severe and complex emotional issues. She also had an extreme alcoholic husband. She would soon have two babies to care for, if she survived the abuse long enough to delivery her unborn baby.

Melbalene did have her baby. Sandy was born before Brenda was even a year old. Where Brenda had been a chunky happy baby, probably due to the wonderful care Melbalene has received while pregnant with Brenda, Sandy was frail and sickly.

Melbalene returned to the tiny mining house, to George and Brenda, with her precious baby girl. She was so grateful to her new friends for taking care of Brenda. Brenda was fascinated with this baby sister and the ladies made such a fuss over Melbalene and her little girls. George was overwhelmed and withdrawn. A drink would be good right about now.

Georges' drinking was out of control. Screaming was heard from the house every evening. His drinking affected his work performance and relations with his friends and coworkers at work. Very soon after the birth of their second daughter, George was let go from the job that he hated at the mine.

The little family soon left the community—where, their friends and neighbors did not know. They wondered what would become of this broken couple, each with their own extreme problem. They wondered even more, what would happen to the precious little girls, less than a year apart in age.

Alone

I recall, even when I was very young, that we moved often. Day to day life was a cycle of extremes. Whatever place we lived in would at times be totally silent. Where were our parents? Then there were the many times there was screaming and crying, running and hiding. Such extremes.

My mother would one day be whistling in the kitchen cooking a meal and the next day screaming and throwing pots, dishes and food against the wall. I was afraid no matter what she was doing. If she was happy, she soon would not be.

My father would go from screaming and hitting my mother to drunk and passed out. He always had a cigarette in his mouth. There was one always just hanging there as he screamed, or smoldering on the floor next to his face when he passed out. Always the rancid smell of alcohol and cigarettes. Always such extremes.

There were also times that he would hold me in his lap and say I was his "sweet soft bunny." He always smelled bad, even right after a bath. As time went on, the foul aroma I associated with my father was the liquor and cigarettes on his breath and in his body.

Sometimes, when he held me, that cigarette would fall out of his mouth onto me and cause a terrible, painful burn. It hurt so much, and I would scream.

My father would immediately stand up and I would fall to the floor. In an instant my father went from sweet talking to screaming at me for crying. Even when things were good, there was anticipation of something inevitably bad.

As I grew older, my understanding was that there were three main reasons we moved so often. My mother would have an emotional break; or my father would have problems at work or lose his job. In either case, we would again move. Sometimes police or social workers would come knocking on the door, and that would hasten the move.

There were rarely other people in our house. It seemed only the four of us, my parents, little sister, Sandy, and myself. If my parents made friends, they were very temporary as they were left behind when we inevitably moved on.

My mother did make friends rather quickly as she was a sweet, outgoing person. Then she would fall apart and become someone very unpredictable. Her friends would stay away. They just didn't know what to think or say. Sometimes her breakdowns were very violent. It could be unsettling, even scary, for grown adults to witness this extreme change in her.

I was alone a lot. In fact, I was alone most of the time, even when my mother was in the house. My father was always gone, sometimes working, sometimes looking for work or sometimes just somewhere else. There were times I was sure my mother was home, but she never seemed to check on me, even when I was very little.

I recall a time I got up early and climbed from my crib. I must have done that often because I did it quickly and easily. I was wandering through the house, but I had a purpose. I was trying to find the place where I played the day before. My mother had played with me—a rare occasion.

I found the place in the house I was looking for. There was a screened-in porch on the back of this house. On the porch were several buckets of water. There were also plastic containers, large spoons and tin cups. My mother had sat on the floor of that porch and played in the water with me.

I had so much fun playing in that water with my mother, I wanted to play again. Suddenly, there was a loud buzzing sound. That sound was not there yesterday when we had played. Then something very painful happened. .

ALONE

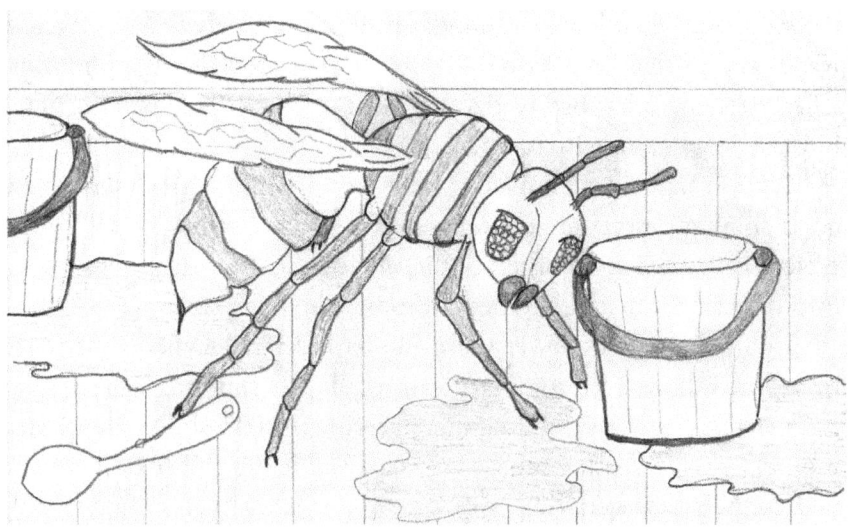

I had gotten stung on my arm. I screamed. I had never gotten stung before. I was soon surrounded by a dozen angry hornets with big yellow faces. They were buzzing all around me and stinging when they landed on me.

I was bitten or stung a number of times. I ran through the house screaming. The stings felt like the cigarette burns I had gotten from my father—so painful. I'd been stung on my face so many times that my eyes were swollen shut. I ran a short distance, screaming and crying, then fell as I couldn't see.

This went on for some time. No one ever came to check on me. Eventually I fell and just stayed there sobbing and crying where I lay. I cried myself to sleep. Then my mother was there and was shaking me. She was shaking me hard and then spanking me saying, "You are a bad girl, Brenda, you woke your sister."

My mother had my six-month-old sister in her arms. When I started to cry again, my little sister cried also. I hurt so much from the hornet stings I didn't even feel the spanking. I was not even two years of age, but this has always been a very clear memory, even today, sixty-five years later.

Well, I guess I was pretty much incorrigible because I was about the same age when I again climbed from my crib. My little sis, Sandy, was asleep in that same crib with me. She was too tiny to climb out. There was also a big bed in that room. It was where my parents slept, but there was no one in that bed.

I was hungry and climbed a chair to reach the table. I was a very good climber despite my chubbiness. There was nothing to eat on the table. I called for my mother, but it seemed she didn't hear me. I went into the bathroom and climbed on top of the toilet seat.

I don't know why I went into the bathroom. Maybe it was potty time, but I didn't go potty that I can recall. The sink was right next to the toilet and as I was standing there peering into the sink, I glimpsed a mouse. I recall that tiny mouse very clearly. He must have been a baby because he was so very tiny

I was thrilled. I was squealing with joy and the baby mouse was squeaking with fear, I'm sure. I leaned against the sink and grabbed that little mouse. He ran between my fingers, squirming and squeaking. He was so tiny, soft and warm. He had huge black eyes, big pink ears and very long whiskers. He was a pretty baby field mouse.

I was giggling and laughing the whole time I played with the tiny mouse. The sound of my laughter bounced around that bathroom and I am sure spilled out into the entire house. I could have played there for hours, and maybe I did. Time flew.

I played with that tiny mouse for such a long time. I was enjoying him so much. Not once did he attempt to bite me. He was even starting to walk right into my hands when I rested my hands quietly and let him. I loved that tiny, downy-soft baby brown mouse.

He very soon was letting me just pet him. He wasn't running away or squeaking at all. He would just sniff my fingers and then look up at me. Field mice are so much prettier than regular ole mice. I was so tickled with this morning adventure I had forgotten how very hungry I was.

My mother was suddenly just there. I was filled with such joy to share the little mouse with her. Just as suddenly as she appeared, she pushed me from the toilet seat, my chunky baby body hitting that tile floor so hard. She scooped up the little mouse and threw him onto the bathroom floor. She quickly stomped on the little creature right there where I was now lying on the floor.

There was so much blood from something so tiny. I was horrified and screaming. She picked him up with a handful of toilet paper and flushed him down the toilet. I stood up and was leaning over the toilet sobbing uncontrollably. I watched that tiny body through my tears, going around and around and finally down the toilet. I had been crying so hard I was now gasping for air as I couldn't breathe.

I could hear my little sis crying from the crib. My mother slapped me so violently I fell back to the floor. She picked me up, shaking me and screaming, "You little brat, now you've woken your sister." My mother left the bathroom. I had the strangest thought and through uncontrolled sobs I suddenly realized I was very hungry.

I recall a game I loved to play with my baby sister, Sandy. It seemed to be just the two of us. I walked slowly backward calling for my little sis, who was just starting to crawl, to follow me. Soon, I was running through the house and she would crawl as fast as she could to catch up with me. I loved that game.

I'd run away from my baby sister a short distance. When I rushed toward her, she'd giggle a wonderful baby giggle. She giggled so hard she couldn't crawl, and she would just roll over. It was so nice to have her to play with.

We played the run and crawl game for what seemed hours. Sometimes I crawled right next to her and she thought this was so funny she would giggle some more. I loved that giggle. I laughed and she would giggle even more. We were such sweet sisters together.

Another incident I recall was once when I was sick. I was in the room on my parents' bed. The crib was in there also, but my sis was not in the crib. It was just me in the room alone. There were no toys, just me sick in my parents' bed. I was so hot from a fever or maybe just the heat, or both.

Their bed was pushed right up against the wall. It was a tight fit in the small room with a bed and a crib. There was also a window on the wall right next to the bed. I was not covered as I was so hot. There was a large spool of bright red thread resting under the windowsill, holding the window open just a couple of inches.

I recall this day very clearly. I remember feeling so hot and thinking that the spool of red thread was so pretty. I do not recall why I started pulling at the spool of thread. Did the pretty red thread get my attention? Was I trying to open the window even more as I felt so hot?

I don't know what possessed me to grab hold of that spool and yank on it so hard that I was able to pull it from under the window. Unfortunately, the window came down on my hand. The spool went flying, end over end, through the air. The bright red thread unreeling from the spool as it flew. On the windowsill, my bright red blood filled the cracks on the wood sill.

I immediately started to scream. The pain was terrible. I could not pull my hand from under the window and I was unable to lift the window off my hand. As I screamed, I heard an echo of my screaming coming from the other side of the door. Somewhere in the house my sis had heard me and was screaming along with me. Mother charged into the room and looked around at the scene.

She saw my hand stuck under the window. She saw the blood on the wood sill. She saw the thread unreeled from the spool. She saw me hysterically trying to pull my hand from under the window. My mother took in the whole scene before her . . . and then she left the room, slamming the door behind her.

I could hear my sister crying from the other room. Her crying was not quite as loud as my screaming. Then I could hear my mother smacking and slapping my little sister and yelling "Just shut up, Sandy, there is nothing wrong with you." Then her screaming echoed mine.

Now both of us girls were screaming and our mother right along with us. I cried myself to sleep with my hand stuck under that window. My mother eventually came back into the room to free me from my trap. I had been crying so hard for so long my eyes were practically swollen shut, but I could tell it was now dark outside.

My fingers were black and blue and terribly swollen. One fingernail was completely torn from a swollen bloody finger. Mother moved me to the crib and then laid my sister next to me. Hand throbbing, I held my little sister close to me. I could hear my father yelling from somewhere in the house.

I was not as alone as I used to be. My little sis was there. We slept in the crib together. We were best of friends. We didn't often see other kids. I was almost a year older. We are always tickled, to this very day, that for twenty-two days every November, we said we were the same age.

I was always a chunky child with straight dark hair and hazel/green eyes. I had fair skin and freckles as I got older. I was even more chunky after my sister was born. If I awoke hungry and there was any milk left in my "best friend's" bottle, I would drink the milk. I no longer got a bottle, but when you're hungry and there's milk in a bottle, you drink it.

Sandy was small, frail and petite, sometimes bordering on scrawny. Me stealing her milk certainly didn't help matters. She cried more than I (maybe she was hungrier). I was usually the one smacked when she cried, even though mother did not know I was stealing her milk.

Sandy had curly blonde hair and big blue eyes. Her eyes looked especially large because her little face was so thin. She seemed to be sick a lot. She couldn't always drink her milk even when she tried to as her "tummy" hurt her. More milk for me!

The thing I liked most about my little sis was that I was not alone. Once she was walking, we were always together. She was a good climber too, so we climbed out of the crib together. Very soon she became faster than I, probably because she was not as chunky.

You would have thought I'd get used to being alone. That was not the case. I was alone before my sister because I had no choice. Once my little sis was here, we had a choice, and we chose to be together.

Sometimes when we awoke, our parents were asleep in the big bed. We never woke them; that could be very scary. Sometimes there was no parent in the room or in the whole house it seemed. But sis and I had each other. We became inseparable, a bond made stronger because of our difficult life.

Very occasionally, family would visit. Some of my mother's siblings were married and had children. Those little cousins would run amuck when they visited us. Sis and I stayed together. Aunts and uncles would comment on how very close we were and say, "Isn't that sweet, the girls are so close." Little did they know.

Sometimes when mother fell apart and had to stay at the hospital, which seemed to happen often, we stayed with family. There was a closeness in our families' homes that we never felt in our own. Our aunts and uncles were so tickled that we fussed so much when it was time to return to our own house. Again, little did they know.

I don't recall my father when he did not smell of liquor. It didn't matter the occasion. When he was passed out on the floor in our house, he smelled of liquor. When we were sitting on his lap as he told us how much he "loved his little darlings," he smelled of liquor. The smells of stale liquor and rancid cigarettes haunted me my whole life.

It was our way of life, constant moving, our mother hospitalized for weeks, sis and I staying with other people, our father drunk, screaming and yelling. Our mother was beat up pretty much every day when she was at home. Perhaps that was how all families were—Sis and I did not know any different.

I wondered, did people around us know of the pain our family endured? Was it the same in other homes? Were we like everyone else, or were we different? We weren't in other homes very often to see how families were.

We had a young aunt (one of Mother's sisters) that stayed with us on occasion. She often witnessed the fights our parents had. One day as a fight started, she put my little sis and me in a stroller and took us for a walk to get all of us away from the screaming.

When we returned to the house, our young aunt found her sister pinned to the floor with our father holding an ice pick to her throat. With all her frightened teenage strength, she pushed our father full force with all her might, right through the front picture window. Our young aunt was never invited to stay with us after that.

I came to know that the closeness between my sis and I was so very strong because we truly only had each other. Sadly, I was thankful that she was with me in this abusive life. My father would often say, "No one needs to know what happens in this house. This family could be separated!" What did that mean? That frightened me so.

Some separations were good. When my father was out of the house, mother was not so nervous, angry and crazy; that was good. When mother was away at the hospital, and we were with family or friends, things were much better. That was good. When sis and I were alone in the mornings, climbing out of our crib together. That was good. I could not imagine being separated from my sis.

At a very young age, if someone, if anyone, for whatever reason asked "Are you okay?" I would always answer that I was. I didn't know any better. I wondered why they would ask such a thing. My father's bellowing rang in my ears, "No one needs to know what happens in this house. This family could be separated!" I was so fearful of that thought.

Together

My sister and I took care of each other. This was the most natural progression, given our family life. My sis would 'mother' me. She fussed over me and was so affectionate. I wondered, where did she get that sweet nature from? She certainly didn't get that from our parents. She was so cute.

Something else was very cute; we looked alike. We were different sizes, with different colored hair and eyes, but our faces were just the same. They were practically interchangeable. We were the "Mr. Potatohead" sisters. From the time we were little until the time we were silver-haired ladies, our faces were the same.

Most times, I, being older, was taking care of her. I was all of three years old and could climb onto a counter 'lickety-split.' Sis could climb just as well but she was too tiny to reach the cupboards. Since I could reach higher, I would often get us breakfast.

After we had breakfast, with our parents usually asleep or gone, we cleaned things up the best we could. We were always making a mess trying to take care of each other. Our mother was so angry with us and our messes. One morning after breakfast, I lifted my sister up onto the toilet seat in the bathroom to help her wash her hands.

Our mother came up behind us and smacked me hard on the back of my head screaming, "I told you not to climb up on that toilet seat."

My chin came down hard on the sink as I was knocked to the floor. My mother grabbed me by my hair and yanked me up off the floor. I held up my arms, covering my face to stave off blows. There was blood everywhere.

Sandy was screaming. I was crying. My father, who was home at the time, joined us in the tiny bathroom. He grabbed my face and tried to clean the blood away with a towel. The more he wiped, the more I bled. "I can see the bone in her chin," my father announced. "We have to take her to the hospital for stitches."

As my father drove us to the hospital my sister continued to cry. I was sitting in my mother's lap. She was pressing the blood-soaked towel to my chin with one hand and slapping my little sister with her free hand screaming, "Stop crying, Sandy, there's nothing wrong with you."

Strangely enough, I was quietly sitting on mother's lap. I was not crying or screaming. I was just sitting in the car tasting blood. I realized that I had also bitten my tongue. My tongue was probably bleeding more than my chin.

There I sat, quietly listening to the chaos around me. My father asked my mother, "Melbalene, what happened?"

My mother answered, "The girls climbed up on the toilet seat and Brenda fell off." Really? My mother had lied!

The nurses at the hospital were very sweet and kind. Both nurses told me how brave I was when the doctor stitched me up. I didn't shed a single tear as he sewed a long line of stitches across my chin. As the doctor left the room, he whispered something to one of the nurses.

The nurse he whispered to came over and gave me a sucker saying, "You can enjoy this when your tongue stops bleeding." There were no stitches in my tongue. I asked the nurse if I could have a sucker for my little sister who was waiting with my parents. "She is not as brave as me," I said, because everyone could hear her crying in the waiting room.

The nurses laughed and one of them gave me an additional sucker. The other nurse inquired "Brenda, how did you get hurt?" I quickly answered, "I fell off. I was bad."

"You weren't bad, sweetheart, it was an accident," one of the nurses said, trying to console me. Once more, little did they know.

There seemed to be no one sheltering us. As I look back it occurs to me that not only were our parents abusive when they had us alone, they were abusive with us in front of each other. Neither of them ever came to our rescue to protect us.

As I mentioned, I tried to take care of Sandy. It did not just happen that way, it was expected. I almost always was the one who got us food when we were hungry, if there was some that I could reach. If my sis would mention to our mother that she was hungry, my mother would slap me saying, "Why didn't you feed your sister?"

When Sandy was about two, it was my responsibility to get her to the toilet when she had to go potty. I was three by that time and am very sure that I had potty-trained myself. No, wait, I was spanked whenever I wet myself. Pain is a powerful teacher.

Now if we were playing, Sandy would forget to tell me she had to pee and she wet herself. If we were some distance from the bathroom and I didn't get her to the toilet quick enough, she wet herself. Other times, while I struggled to pick my sis up and sit her on the toilet, she would wet on the floor.

I am very sure that I was slapped or spanked more times potty training my little sis than I ever was potty training myself. Just to be clear, there was no potty. There was only the full-sized toilet in the bathroom, so not only did I have to get her up on the toilet. I had to hold onto her so she would not fall in.

Sandy was tiny and I was not very strong. No matter how careful I was, she did fall into the toilet on several occasions. Getting her out of the toilet was more difficult than getting her on the toilet.

It seemed to take a very long time for my little sis to get the idea of going pee in the toilet instead of her panties, or heaven forbid, the floor. One day I was frantically trying to find something to clean up her latest "pee puddle." I held my sister's hand as we walked toward a closet to find a rag to clean up with.

Suddenly my mother grabbed me by my hair, yanked me off the floor and pulled me to the still warm puddle of urine. She pushed my face straight down into that warm urine yelling, "Brenda, this is your mess, now clean it up." I was trying to clean it up!

As I was gasping violently, my face pressed hard against the floor, I could feel the warm liquid going up my nose and down my throat. I was horrified, coughing and choking. My little sis was right there, of course, and started to cry. Mother, as usual, slapped Sandy and screamed, "Stop your crying, Sandy, there is nothing wrong with you."

Of course, there was something wrong with Sandy. As with every other time my sister saw me abused, she was deeply affected by it. When I was hurt, she cried. When I was slapped, she cried. And when I cried, we wept in unison. There was most definitely something horribly wrong.

There was another recollection of Sandy and me playing together. A house that we lived in had two floors, with the bedrooms upstairs. Sandy and I were about three and four. We were putting dirty clothes in a large laundry bag to take to the basement to be washed.

We had an idea for an exciting game we could play. I encouraged my little sister to crawl into the laundry bag and I pulled her down the stairs. I pulled her to the landing with her giggling at every bounce on the way down the stairs. Then we switched places. Sandy pulled me to the next landing. I laughed so hard. This game was so much fun.

At the bottom of the stairs, we both grabbed hold of the laundry bag, ran giggling to the top of the stairs and started our silly game over again. About the third time, when I was in the laundry bag, I heard my mother come to the stairs and start screaming at my sister. Then my mother was screaming for me to get out of the laundry bag.

As I struggled to free myself from the bag, mother started to kick me. I could not get out of the laundry bag, and I could not get away. I lay curled up in that bag as my mother walked around it and kicked me from all sides. Sandy was screaming. I was in the bag crying and struggling to get out. Then suddenly, I was bleeding. My mother had kicked me square in the face. My nose was bleeding profusely.

My mother opened the laundry bag and yanked me out by my hair. My mouth was full of blood and my face was completely bloody. Blood was everywhere, on the bag and puddled on the floor. Sandy was screaming, I was crying, and mother was yelling. Just then my father came into the room reeking of liquor.

My father was cussing as he took in the scene. "What the hell happened, Melbalene"? Mother screamed back, "Stupid ass Sandy was pulling Brenda down the stairs in the laundry bag and bloodied her nose."

Of course, she lied. We were both spanked and sent to our room. At least we were together. I buried my face in a pillow to cover the sound of my crying and to stop the bleeding. We cried ourselves to sleep.

Besides being good climbers, as time went on, we became good runners also. If our mother started screaming and yelling, we ran. Probably because it was inevitable that one or both of us was going to get a beating. It didn't make a difference if we had done something wrong; mother was screaming, so there would be a beating.

One day, and I don't recall what happened to anger my mother (maybe nothing), she started screaming. My sis and I were in the front yard playing. We immediately stood up from the grass where we were sitting and ran toward the back yard. The back yard was fenced in and I ran to the fence and scurried over.

Now this was called a cyclone fence. It was intertwined steel pieces. Usually the barbed sharp points along the top of these fences were bent down. On this fence, however, the barbed points were sticking dangerously up on the top row. While climbing over the fence, I got terribly cut up. Deep scratches on my arms and legs were bleeding.

Sandy was right behind me. Just as she started to climb up over the dangerous, spiky barbed top, mother grabbed her by her legs. In trying to stop Sandy, our mother pulled with all her strength on Sandy's legs. As she was pulled downward, the pointed barbed fencing on that top row went right through the tender skin of her underarm.

Sandy let out a blood-curdling scream. I don't know if our mother knew that the barbed spikes had punctured my sister's underarm, but I do know that my mother kept pulling, and pulling even more. The screaming had caused a ruckus and a neighbor called the police.

By this time, I had run around the house and was standing beside mother. I was crying to see my sister's pain. My sis was crying and whimpering pitifully. Blood was starting to drip down the fence and puddle on the ground.

My little sis was in agony. When the police arrived, they found mother trying to get my sister off the top spiked row of the fence. Her skin and the barbs were a tangled mess. The police called an ambulance for medical help.

While waiting for help to arrive, one of the policemen held my sister in his arms up close to the top of the fence. He was quietly trying to comfort and console her so she would stop struggling. Every time she kicked or squirmed the sharp barbs went deeper into her skin.

The other policeman was speaking with mother and asked her what had happened. Mother explained, "Sandy was climbing over the fence when Brenda grabbed her by the legs and tried to pull her down." My mother had lied! She lied about me right to the policeman. He looked at me quite concerned.

I heard mother's explanation. What could I say? I said nothing. The policeman knelt in front of me and took my shaking hands in his.

"You need to be more careful with your little sister. I know you didn't intend to hurt her," he said quietly, wiping away my tears. I just stood before him with more tears streaming down my face. There was nothing I could say. He put his arms around me, and I cried even more.

When the medical team arrived, they took Sandy off the barbed points. It was not easy, and it took quite a while. She cried through the whole process and was soon completely exhausted. A neighbor man had showed up and was turning down the points in the top row of the fence with some type of tool. It wasn't even his fence. The policemen thanked him.

My sister was taken to the hospital. We were told she would be at the hospital for several days. When my father came home that evening, my mother told him her version of the story. It was the same lie she had told the policeman. My father was very upset that I had hurt my little sister. I was slapped across the face and then spanked. I cried myself to sleep, alone in the crib, missing my sister.

I was heartbroken that my sister was hurt, and we were separated. I was even more heartbroken that mother had told the policeman and my father that I'd hurt my little sister. The very next day my parents and I went to the hospital to visit Sandy and maybe bring her home. I was so excited to be with her again.

Sandy was a very pretty and enchanting little girl. She was tiny, with big blue eyes and long curly, bouncy blonde hair. She was very friendly and talkative with all the hospital staff. She was sweet and was enjoying all this attention. The nurses loved her as she chattered away in her cute baby talk.

The nurses had given Sandy little gifts to cheer her up. She had candy, little bows for her hair and a tiny kewpie-doll (a silly plastic doll that was very popular when sis and I were young). With every gift they gave her she would thank them and say "for my Sissy."

Now the nurses knew the story mother told of how Sandy had gotten her injuries. They were so surprised that this sweet little girl was saving her gifts for the sister that had been the cause of her injury. When they tried to encourage her to eat the candy or enjoy her dolly,

Sandy would simply say in her three-year-old baby like voice, "They're for Sissy."

"Sissy" was the pet name we called each other.

As years went by there was so much that we both knew and had experienced together. We kept so much from other people, but we shared everything with each other. It was nice not to be alone in this sad and violent childhood, but what a pitiful force bound us together and kept us so close.

Strangely enough, mother and father were so proud of us girls whenever the family was in public. Sandy and I were the best-behaved children, and people would often comment on exactly that. They would also comment on how devoted we were to each other and that our mother and father must be wonderful parents to have such obedient daughters. Just how had they managed to raise us that way? I don't recall their answer. Sis and I knew. Pain is a powerful teacher.

As mentioned, sis and I were told regularly that what happened in our house was no one's business. Sandy and I were both also extremely careful. We never shared anything that happened in our house; the threat of being separated was more frightening to us than the abuse itself.

There were good moments and even pleasant days with each other, and rarely even with our parents. Wherever we lived, and we moved often, our mother kept the house very nice. It was always clean and organized. Our mother was also a wonderful cook. And when we went anywhere, sis and I were cleaned and dressed so pretty. Our father bought us matching dresses as if we were twins. It was strange though.

My father also bought beautiful dresses for our mother. I don't recall her ever shopping for her own clothes when we were young. Father liked her dressed nice and insisted she look good when he came home from work. Whatever she might be doing during the day, she would give herself plenty of time to "look pretty for your Daddy."

Mother made friends quickly. She was a friendly and sweet person and people were drawn to her. She had a childlike quality in some ways, so open and honest. She was extremely easy to talk to and seemed to be so very compassionate.

She looked to be a beautiful woman inside and out. She was truly beautiful. She had dark eyes and thick wavy dark hair well past her shoulders. She was thin and shapely. She wore red lipstick that our father really liked as he said, "on her pouty lips."

Our father was a handsome man. He was tall and slender with bright blue eyes. He really liked fancy men's clothing. As nice as the dresses were that he bought for our mother and for us, his own clothing was always the best of the best. When our family was in public, people watched us walk by. We were picture perfect. The truth, of course, was not pretty.

People also always commented on how smart and handy our father was. They came to him for help with just about any problem they had at their homes. He seemed to know how to fix anything. He really was very intelligent. To the outside world, he was the nicest and sweetest man. To the outside world he was a devoted husband and a loving father. The perfect facade was far from the horrible reality.

Father could also be very affectionate with Sandy and me. He would sit us on his lap and tell us how sweet and pretty his girls were. He mostly did this when there were other people around. His attention just reinforced the false vision people had of our family. Sandy and I enjoyed this attention; it was safe in front of other people.

But things were not as they appeared. Neighbors that we became friends with were always so shocked when the facade inevitably fell apart. Our mother's sanity was very precarious, and our father could only pose as a sober, loving husband and father for a short time.

Our life with our parents was a strange cycle of extremes, whether in private or in the eyes of the public. Pretty as we may have looked to the outside world, we were two little girls so broken and damaged on the inside. We held our breath when things seemed good, because something awful would soon happen.

Damaged

Our parents did not complement each other in their damaged relationship. Strangely, they almost seemed too close. If one grew depressed the other would also become depressed. They were a mutual yoyo. When one was up the other was up and happy. When one was angry or upset, the other would soon follow suit.

They were no "yin-yang couple" where opposite forces complement one another, or one would offset the other's shortcomings, moods or character. Of course, their yoyo relationship created the inevitable roller coaster world that we survived together when my sister and I were young.

Mother was abused regularly; she was slapped and beaten often by father. She was knocked to the floor, kicked and pulled by her hair. Sis and I always cowered somewhere together. Hiding was a natural and normal part of our days. Didn't other children hide in fear of their parents?

There were times when mother heard our father cussing and stumbling drunk up the stairs, and she would say, "Girls, go hide." This was not a game of hide and seek. This was a matter of life and death.

Sis and I were about three and four when our poor mother was again most severely beaten by our father. It was probably the worst we had ever seen, not counting possibly worse beatings of which we were not aware. Mother told us to hide and we were obediently hiding in a clothes hamper.

We never did look, but the sounds were terrible. First, she cried "Please George, don't," and then there was a terrible loud slapping sound and a more muffled punching sound, over and over. These were the things that night terrors were made of.

Between heartbreaking, pitiful sobs she would beg not to be hit anymore. Then you could hear the air escape her as she was either punched or kicked in the stomach. We didn't know because we weren't watching. Not this time anyway. Just hearing this was beyond traumatizing. The sound of silence afterwards was even more frightening.

Then we could hear something being dragged through the house. We knew it was our mother. Other than the sound of dragging, everything was deathly silent. The silence was sickening. We could hear the closet door being opened—it had a very distinctive squeak, and then the loud slam of the closet door.

Our father walked around the house for just a very short time calling us. "Where are my pretty girls? Where are my sweet soft darlings?" We heard him fall to the floor, passed out, we were sure. We stayed hidden for what seemed like hours. Then the sound of loud snoring filled the house.

Sis and I climbed slowly from our hiding place in the hamper. We snuck past our unconscious father. He lay there on the floor, a cigarette bouncing on his lip with every snore. The rancid smell of old liquor rose from his smelly unconscious body. We quietly tip-toed to the closet.

We could just barely reach the doorknob, but we could not reach the lock far up on the door. We were too frightened to attempt to pull a chair to the closet to reach the lock, for fear of awakening our drunken father. We sat together on the floor holding each other, leaning against that closet door. We cried ourselves to sleep with big silent tears. No sound came from within the closet.

I don't recall just what happened later. How long did we sit sleeping by that closet door? When did our father wake up? How did our mother get out of the closet? I don't know. I do know that some days later, maybe even weeks, our mother had one of her very worst mental breakdowns. She beat us everytime we came near her, passing on the abuse she received. We tried to stay away from mother. She was soon hospitalized and was gone for weeks.

I know my little sis and I were traumatized, this time more acutely. When your life is a series of heartbreaks, you may get numb to the abuse for a while, and then it gets worse. Bigger abuse, bigger heartbreak, bigger trauma, bigger bruises. The abuse reaches your core where it twists and changes you.

I don't recall where we stayed while she was away at the hospital after this, worse than usual, breakdown. Friends or family, I don't know. Maybe we were just home alone. I blanked out that couple of weeks from my traumatized thoughts, as did my sister. I do know that when mother returned to us, she did not know us for a long time. She did not even know our names.

This was an entirely different kind of heartbreak, when your mother doesn't know you. It was as if she had to relearn her life, her sad abusive life. Just in time for our family to cross into something worse than ever.

Our father drank more, if that was even possible. Our mother was more unstable, with less and less good days. We moved so often the boxes were rarely unpacked and the houses no longer seemed organized or clean. The meals mother made were pitiful, halfhearted attempts to quickly feed us.

We had more visitors though—usually police, ladies from social services or big angry men. Years later I was told my father stole from companies he worked for, or just stole, so there were police. I was told he had a criminal record of drunk and disorderly, petty theft and breaking into homes. Debts were not always paid, we just moved. Those big angry men were bill collectors.

Our parents didn't make friends like they used to in the past. I don't know if they even tried. First, we moved too quickly, and neighbors would see police at whatever house we were staying. Not exactly the best way to make friends and meet the neighbors.

Our mother was more out of touch. Perhaps too much medication, or not enough. She was so withdrawn and alone, even with her daughters there with her. She needed a strong, caring person in her life; little girls can't fill that void and really shouldn't be expected to.

Our father became a different kind of scary. Where he once would pull both my sis and I up onto his lap and tell us we were "daddy's sweet, soft babies" or "daddy's precious little girls" (always with smelly liquor breath), now he got us alone. It's a strange combination of fear and love. You love your father but being alone with him is very fearsome and uncomfortable.

Something very sad was happening between my sis and myself. I was five with my sister a year younger. Our father always said, "No one needs to know what happens within this family or they will separate us." Sandy and I always shared everything we went through. We never shared anything we went through with anyone else, but we always did with each other. Now my father would tell me, "Don't tell anyone, not even your sister or your mother."

I was frightened and very alone with this new threat looming. But still, I did as I was told. My father would hold me on his lap with no one else in the room. He would stroke my hair and call me his "soft bunny," his foul liquor breath overpowering my senses. I recall liking the attention but feeling strangely uncomfortable with him. I also caught my father with my little sis.

She would be sitting on Father's lap just giggling and smiling. I could not always hear what he was saying to her, but I could smell him from my hiding place. I once heard him call her his "sweet little snatch." I never did know what he meant by that phrase.

When I would see my father with my sister, I think I felt a twinge of jealousy. But then again, I didn't want to be on his lap, it scared me so. Now I was afraid for my sister; I didn't want her on his lap either. Everything was so confusing.

Things got worse in other ways. I can close my eyes and see the scenes playing out like a movie, but I don't like to relive the scenes. One beautiful summer day, my mother took my sis and me for a walk. Sis and I held hands and skipped along, laughing and singing silly songs. It was a perfectly beautiful day and even our mother's eyes were sparkling.

As we got closer to the house where we were living, some little neighbor kids came running up to us. They were so excited, but they were very difficult to understand. They were younger than us and it was pretty much baby gibberish. We did understand that their excitement had something to do with a puppy.

When we got to the house there was a box on the porch. According to Mother someone had written on the box "for Brenda and Sandy." Sis and I were so tickled. Our mother lifted the puppy from the box and handed him to us. A beautiful puppy! Our mother was so tickled and was laughing as we giggled with joy.

We were squealing with delight. Our mother was smiling and laughing. The little neighbor kids were as excited as we were. That little pup was a beige color with long ears and big beautiful dark brown eyes. His hair was rather long and wavy. He had a short little tail that could not wag enough to show his own excitement, so his entire puppy butt wagged side to side.

Us kids would run, and he would chase. We would fall on the grass and that little pup would give us puppy kisses, puppy butt wagging the whole time. He would run from sis and back to me, and from kid to kid, his happy mouth in a full puppy grin. My mother was laughing out loud, I don't think I'd ever heard that before.

I did not know I could feel so happy. I looked at my little sis so joyful and my mother smiling as she watched us play. That beautiful sunny day suddenly became completely horrific in a way I could never have imagined.

My father pulled up the gravel driveway in his old beat-up truck. My mother was so excited to tell him what a nice idea it was for him to get the puppy for us girls. That is where she thought the puppy came from because who else would have done it?

Before she could say a word, our father screamed, "Where in the hell did that dog come from?"

Our mother replied, "Someone left it in a box for the girls, I thought it was from you."

"The last thing we need is a damn dog," our father snarled even louder, his face red, fists clenched.

Father pulled a length of rope from the back of his truck. He grabbed up the frightened little puppy (cowering from the loud screaming) and tied the rope around its tiny neck. He tied the other end of the rope to the back bumper of his truck. Our father jumped into his truck and drove away, so fast the little beige pup with the beautiful dark brown eyes was dragged behind the speeding truck.

Everyone was shocked and crying. Sis and I were crying on the porch in our mother's arms, tears rolling down her face and sobs escaping from her throat. The little neighbor kids were running home, crying as they ran, their baby gibberish anguished nonsense.

We stayed on the porch with our mother until it was dark. The old beat-up truck finally pulled into the driveway. In the glow of the streetlight we could see the puppy still tied to the back bumper of the truck. The puppy lay there on the gravel driveway, not moving. Our mother walked to the truck. She peered inside to see our father was passed out against the steering wheel. He was, of course, drunk.

She went to the back of the truck. In the glow of the streetlight we saw our mother pick up the dead puppy. She sat there in the dark, in the dirt and gravel of the driveway holding the pup in her arms crying and rocking back and forth. Sis and I walked into the house hand in hand and climbed into our crib. Our beautiful day had ended so cruelly.

As an adult, pets and animals in general have always brought me great joy. This was a passion that I did not inherit from my parents. When I was older and stayed on my grandparents' farm, I learned to love God's gift of animals. But stories were very different where my parents were concerned.

I was almost five years old when we moved into a house with an old garage or barn-like structure in the back of the very big yard. My sis and I loved to explore around and inside that old building. Now, of course, we would sneak in, which was easy as there was no mother in sight and no father around to stop us.

One day while exploring in the old building, Sandy and I heard a low, quiet squeaking sound. We searched everywhere but could not locate where the sound was coming from. After a couple days we returned to the old building. We followed the squeaking sound more easily as it seemed to be louder. We found something special. A litter of tiny kittens, six furry babies, in an old beat-up dresser drawer pulled halfway out from the dresser.

They were each a different color. There was a black, a gray, a yellow striped, a black with white paws, a gray with white paws and a gray striped. We were so excited. We sat there and watched them squeak, meow and wiggle around. Their eyes were not yet opened.

We picked them up and held them in our laps. They were so snuggly and cuddly. They would suck on our pinky fingers and push against us with their tiny kitty paws. They would make these strange little purr/growl sounds as they sucked our fingers.

It was our secret. We found time to visit them every day. One day while we were visiting, a large gray cat showed up and was growling at us. The cat would take a couple steps toward us then stop and growl. We were pretty sure those kittens were hers, or his.

We put the kittens down and slowly backed away from the old dresser and the angry gray cat. That large gray cat jumped into that drawer and those kittens were all over her. They were sucking on her belly just as they had sucked on our fingers, pushing with their tiny paws. We watched for a short time and finally left her with the kittens.

We decided to continue to visit the kittens, but we would just watch them. With that big gray cat growling we were sure she did not like us holding her kittens. That was our plan when each day we went into the old building to "just watch" the precious furry family. Well, that plan did not work. One day, the kittens saw us just standing there and they jumped out of the dresser drawer and walked right over to us, meowing with every tiny step! They walked to us! It was so cute!

We visited them quickly and left before big gray cat came back to scold us. The next day I was going to start school, the first time ever. I was so nervous to go to school. I would miss my sister. I told her when I came home from my first day at school, we would go together to visit our kitten family. "Please wait for me, sissy," I pleaded.

On my first day of school I sat in the back. The kids were seated by their last name and my name was at the end of the alphabet. I was too shy to even raise my hand when my name was called. I had long straight dark hair and sat quietly in my chair with my face hidden behind my hair.

My favorite part of my school day was walking home with a little neighbor girl. She had laughed and giggled all day and made friends with so many kids at school. I didn't make any friends, but that little girl was so sweet with me and held my hand and walked me home.

I couldn't wait to see my little sister and tell her about school. I couldn't wait until she and I could sneak to see our kittens. Suddenly, to my shock, my mother grabbed me by the hair as soon as I came into the house. She was shaking me and screaming at me: "You got your sister hurt really bad. What is wrong with you that you would do such a thing?" I was slapped. I had no idea what was happening.

I ran to the bedroom, and there was my sister, covered with deep scratches. There were red swollen, nasty scratches on her face. They were on her arms, her legs and even on her back. They looked terrible, all red and puffy like that. She cried when she saw me. "I'm sorry, Sissy, please don't be mad at me!" What?

As it turned out, Sandy just could not wait until I came home from school to visit our kittens in the old building. She went into the old building to just stand and watch them for a while. Those kittens ran right to her! She said they were so cute. They ran to her and she couldn't resist just sitting with them and holding them for just a minute.

While she was with the kittens, she heard a low, angry growl. When she glanced around, there were several, big scary cats growling at her. She got up to run but they went after her and she was knocked down or fell and was terribly scratched before she could get away. "I'm so sorry, I should have waited for you like you asked." I felt so bad. We cried.

The next day was not a school day. Sis felt just fine, the scratches didn't really hurt any more, but they did look terrible. She was a little nervous but determined to see our kittens. We snuck out to the old building and pushed our way through the old broken door. We would be very careful to leave quickly if those big mean cats showed up. We did not hear any growling cats. We also did not hear the kittens.

The drawer was empty where they usually were. Perhaps after the incident, the kittens had left. Perhaps those big cats had even taken them away since the kittens could now climb and run. We were sad that we could not see them. They had been so sweet. We had looked forward to visiting them, even after Sandy was attacked.

We walked through the building for a while looking all around. We called for the kittens, not even fearful of the cats. We were so determined to find our six furry friends. We did finally hear something. It was the sound of that old broken door opening.

We both turned toward the door and saw our mother. She was walking into the old building clumsily carrying a large heavy bucket. "Here's your damn kittens," she said as she set the heavy bucket on the floor. She turned and left the building.

We were both so excited. We ran to the door and looked in the bucket, and there were our kittens. They were all floating dead in a bucket filled with water. We just stood there, peering into that water. We were holding hands, and both started shaking uncontrollably. We weren't even crying, just shaking.

We walked to the front yard together, hand in hand, and sat in the grass. We sat there a long time and soon started to cry, ever so quietly. We held each other and decided, as much as we hated the idea, we would go back to the old building and bury our dead kittens.

We returned to the old building. That bucket was nowhere in sight. We really didn't want to touch the dead, wet kittens, but this was even worse. We did look for the bucket to no avail.

We finally left the building, never to return. We didn't dare ask our mother anything about our kittens, not ever. Our father was not home that day, just our mother. To think she had drowned those sweet baby kittens, it made us sick, physically and mentally.

Desperate

I couldn't see anything, it was absolutely, pitch-black. I knew where I was—I'd been here before, many times. I was locked in a closet with my sister. I'd been here often enough to have memorized everything around me.

There were shelves built into the walls. There were various cleaning products on the shelves. The closet smelled of chemicals, especially something called Murphy's Oil Soap. The smell of that product always made me sick. There was an old rusty bucket on the floor. There was a smelly, damp mop next to the bucket.

There were spider webs on the ceiling, homes of big black spiders. There were dust webs on the shelves, often referred to as 'dust bunnies.' There was a little hole chewed through one baseboard where mice ran in and out, scurrying and squeaking.

I knew there was a broom, a dust mop and a canister vacuum cleaner on a large shelf. I'm sure the nozzle hung off the shelf as did the long water hose that sat on the shelf right next to it. There was an old wooden box full of rags for dusting and cleaning.

I knew there were work jackets hanging on hooks on the wall and a pair of work boots on the floor. I couldn't see them, but I knew they were there. These were giant work boots, almost as tall as I was as I sat there on the floor. Oh wait, they were not truly giant boots, my little sis and I were small, just four and five years of age.

DESPERATE

There was a pee puddle on the floor—oh no, not again. I couldn't see it, but I could smell it. I could smell the damp mop and some of the chemicals. All these smells made me so nauseous. Oh, I hoped I wouldn't throw up. I'd done that in the past from the smells or the fear of the dark closet.

I could hear things. I heard my heart beating in my chest. I heard my little sister breathing gently on the floor next to me, an occasional sob escaping from her throat. She'd cried herself to sleep—had it been hours now?

I could feel things. I felt the rough, splintery wood floor beneath us. I felt the shelves against my back. I felt my little sister's head resting on my lap, her hair sweaty and in damp curly ringlets from the heat of the closet.

Oh no, I touched that pee puddle. I didn't intend to touch it. Yuk. My little sis couldn't help herself as we'd been in here such a long time. I would be punished for the pee puddle. At least my sister would not be hurt, maybe.

If there were lights on in the room outside the closet, the light would come under the door and light things up with a dim eerie glow.

The light would also stream through the keyhole, but there was no light. The room on the other side of the door was dark.

If our parents had been in that room, there would be more arguing and fighting. That is when we were most often locked in a closet. To hide us or punish us? I don't know which, I never did. I heard not a single sound from the other side of the door. I was okay with the silence, but the pitch black of the closet made me nervous.

If just one of our parents was in the room, it would have been our mother. Our father would have stormed out of the house cussing and swearing. She would have been crying alone in the room. She would always cry after they fought. She was often beat up and hit hard during these fights. Makeup did not always cover her black eyes and bruises the next day when she tried to make herself "look pretty for your Daddy."

When I got home from school today my parents were fighting. Across the room my little sis was standing up against the closet door crying. I walked around my angry, fighting parents to get to my sister. My father took a couple steps toward me just as I got to my sister. We both ran into the closet. Someone pushed the door closed and hooked the latch at the top of the door.

We must have been locked in the closet for hours. I realized I was very hungry. We were locked in here just after school. It was now dark and silent in the closet, and in the room outside the closet. Now I could also hear my stomach growling. To make matters worse, I had to pee.

How sad that I was okay within the pitch dark and eerily silent closet. There were things much more frightening in our young lives than a dark closet. That closet was a short reprieve from what it could be. Oh no . . . I did finally hear something, footsteps from bare feet. There was the sound of a light switch being flicked on. It made such a loud click in the silence.

Light streamed under the door and through the keyhole. The muffled footsteps were coming closer. There was the sound of the latch being unhooked. Someone was turning the handle on the closet. The sound woke my little sister and she immediately started to cry. The closet door creaked open. We tried to adjust our huge scared eyes to the light streaming into the closet.

Whether it was our mother or father, I was very sure things were going to go from dark and silent to scary and painful. I wish I could protect my little sister, but I was just one year older. I was five years of age and so helpless to do anything, except hold my little sis close when she later cried herself to sleep, again.

Our mother stepped into the closet. She did not say a word. She did not come closer to us. She did not scream, shake us or hit us. She certainly didn't hug us. Her dress was torn, and her hair was a mess, some of it stuck to her face with blood. There were bruises and marks on her face and arms, there almost always were.

She looked at us quickly and turned and walked away. We followed her to the bedroom. She fell into her bed, crying into her pillow. Sis followed me as I climbed into the crib (yes, we still shared the old crib). I no longer had to pee. I had done that when the closet door opened. We lay cuddled together in the crib. We were both so hungry but did eventually fall asleep to the sound of growly stomachs and our mother's crying.

This was our young life. I guessed that every kid at school could have a life like this. Maybe this is perfectly normal. I didn't know any different. I didn't make friends at school. I never talked to the other kids. I was often late for school or would miss days altogether. I never explained to anyone why.

I was always afraid to be away from my sister. I would be lost in thought and didn't hear the teacher when she spoke to me or called my name. I was often in trouble for this reason. I just went to school as I was told I had to and waited to go home.

Notes were written by the teacher for me to take home. I don't know what the teacher wrote, but every time I took a note home I was spanked. Every time I was spanked my sister would cry. Every time my sister would cry, my mother would spank her also. These weren't little taps on the butt with her palm. They almost always left huge red welts from a belt.

We were also often hit with a switch, a skinny branch cut from a tree. Wherever we were, we were told to go find a tree and break off a switch. What a very cruel thing to ask a child to do. We would pick a very flimsy branch for our punishment.

Our mother then went out herself and picked a different switch—a long, scary mean-looking branch. It sounded like a whip when snapped in the air. These would sometimes cause bloody streaks across our backs.

What could little girls ages four and five possibly do that was bad enough to warrant this extreme punishment. We were so fearful all the time of the parents we wanted to love. There was so much emotional confusion in our lives every day.

Our mother screamed at me saying, "If you don't pay attention at school, they may send someone to the house to check on us. If someone checks on us, this family will be separated." This was something our father had always told us; now our mother was saying the same thing. The threat was more frightening to me than the beatings.

Our father was hardly ever home now. That was probably a good thing as there would be even more screaming and yelling if he was. Late one evening, after sis and I fell asleep, I heard voices. We were always told not to leave our crib until morning. But when the voices went on and on, I climbed from the crib to find out what was going on.

I went quietly to the front room. My mother was sitting in a chair crying very softly. My father was on the floor in front of her, on one knee. He was saying, "Boots, honey I love you. You know I love you, baby. Please don't cry, everything will be okay, please forgive me Boots." I stared at this scene in disbelief. I was so confused to see my parents like this.

I had never seen any kind of affection between my parents. He leaned forward and took my mother's face between his hands. He was kissing her face over and over and after each kiss would say, "I will never hit you again baby, I promise." He went on talking through his tears, "You and our girls mean everything to me; you know that." He sounded so desperate and sincere.

DESPERATE

He pulled her right down on the floor with him and held her in his arms. I was watching this scene and crying. I didn't understand at all what I was seeing. He held her in his arms there on the floor and they both cried. He was so sweet and gentle with my mother. I had never seen them like this before.

I went back to the bedroom and climbed into the crib. I wanted to wake my sister and take her to the front room. I wanted sis to see what our parents were doing. I was so scared and confused, I didn't wake Sandy. That sweet gentle scene stuck in my mind. It was such a foreign contrast to our lives.

Not very long after I discovered my father kneeling on the floor crying for my mother to forgive him, Mother did something I did not understand for a very long time. She spent a good amount of time one day fussing over Sandy and me. She gave us a bath first thing in the morning, right after our father left the house! She dressed us in our prettiest matching dresses. She fixed our hair so special.

She kept smiling this nervous smile the entire time. She kept kissing our faces and hugging us. So unlike her. She put on our very nice "special occasion" jackets and our pretty shiny black shoes. Sis and I were so tickled; we looked wonderful. Mother then announced that we were going for a nice walk. It turned out to be a very long walk.

We lived in Cleveland at that time. We had often passed a very large stone building with lots of trees in the gated yard. The building with the trees around it was very pretty. There was a very large rock, as big as a bus, in the front of the building with words carved in the stone. We couldn't yet read words. Sis and I had always noticed the building and the yard and were always curious.

Mother opened the gate which was taller than she was. She took our hands and the three of us walked up the long winding sidewalk, right up to the steps in front of the building. Mother started to cry. She hugged both of us and through tears said, "I want you girls to sit here and wait until someone comes to get you. Be very good girls, like I know you can be."

Of course, we did as we were told. My little sis, Sandy, and I sat on those steps. We sat on those steps for a very long time. We did not get up. We were told to sit. We sat there in the sunlight and then in the darkness. We were being the very good girls our mother knew we could be.

We were getting hungry, but we were used to being hungry. We both had to go potty, but there was no potty. We sat and sat, but no one came. We sat closer together because it was getting cold. If someone came, they couldn't even see how wonderful sis and I looked, because it was now dark outside. No one came.

Then we saw someone walking along the winding sidewalk. It was a woman and she was walking right to us. We didn't know if we should be excited or scared. It was very dark, and we could not see her very well. She came right up to us and suddenly scooped us up into her arms. It was our mother.

Years later, we again had the opportunity to drive past the beautiful stone building with the tall wrought iron gate and pretty trees and the large engraved rock the size of a bus. We were older and could read the lettering engraved on the huge rock. It said *Orphanage*! Our mother confessed to us many years later that she had come very close to giving us up that day. She said she was afraid for us.

DESPERATE

The winter after this adventure, we started to get a lot of company. It was close to the holidays when the company started to show up. It was not a good thing. The first was a woman who said the school had asked her to come visit us. I had missed a lot of classes and she wanted to be sure things were okay at home.

My mother called sis and me into the room to speak with the woman. I didn't like this strange woman; she made me very nervous, even scared. She had very curly, very red hair and thick eyeglasses with dark rims. She smiled the whole time with her very big horse teeth that hardly fit in her mouth. She was nice enough, but I was suspicious. Was she going to separate our family?

The woman smiled at Sandy and me and asked how we were doing. Of course, we told her we were just fine. What else could we say? She didn't ask anything real specific, but the answer would be the same, we were just fine.

When she left, my mother became very angry at me. She shook me hard and slapped my face. Mother said that I had better be especially good at school. This was my fault; if I had been good the lady would not have come to the house.

A couple of days later a very angry man came to the door. He was yelling at my mother about the money for the rent. I had never seen my mother getting screamed and yelled at by anyone except my father. It was the strangest thing that mother did not cry.

She stood firm and strong in front of that big, angry man. She told him she would have her husband take care of the problem and asked the big, mean man to leave the house. "Please leave, now," she told him forcefully. He quickly left the house.

Then someone came to the house that was even stranger than the woman from school and the man about the rent. Our very own father. It was strange because he came to the house one day with a Christmas tree. A Christmas tree, really! We had never had a Christmas tree!

It was a tiny tree, but it was so beautiful. It was small and he placed it on the table. It was covered with colorful lights and shiny gold bows. It was our first ever Christmas tree. Father left the house for just a moment.

When he returned, he carried in three boxes wrapped in pretty paper with ribbons. They were Christmas presents for us! We had never had Christmas presents, not ever! There was a box for my sister, a box for me and a big box for our mother. There was also a fourth box and it had food in it! There was crackers and cheese. There were apples and cookies. There were packs of luncheon meats and bread. It was a Christmas feast!

Sandy and I were overjoyed. We were jumping up and down squealing and laughing. Christmas, a real Christmas. I didn't know what to think. Sis and I opened our presents at the same time. Inside the boxes were big, beautiful baby dolls. We had never had baby dolls before. They looked the same, both with blue bonnets and blue britches. They each had a baby doll bottle. We didn't mind that they were the same, we were so thrilled.

Sis and I named our baby dolls right then and there. We didn't even have to think about it. Sandy named hers Billy and I named mine Bobby. I don't know how we came up with the names so quickly, but we did. We were so happy. (Something strange about those baby doll names . . . fifty years later my sis married a man named Billy and I married a man named Bobby, our last of many husbands.)

Mother was just getting ready to open her present. It was a large box with shiny paper and lots of ribbons. She was teary-eyed and so very tickled and happy. She set the large box on her lap and smiled up at our father. There was a look of joy and love on her face we had never seen. It was a precious moment.

Just then there was loud banging on the door. Our father went to the door, angrily cussing that this special moment was so rudely interrupted. He yanked open the door. Suddenly two policemen charged into the house. They put handcuffs on our father. Mother was trying to push the policemen away from our father. Then three more men came into the house.

One man grabbed up the Christmas tree and snatched up the box with our Christmas feast. We hadn't even had one bite of food. One of the men grabbed the large box from the floor where mother had dropped it. The last man to come into the house walked right up to my sis and I and snatched the baby dolls and their baby bottles right from our hands.

He did not say a word and he didn't even look at us. He took Billy and Bobby. Our first ever baby dolls were just gone. The men left the house with our Christmas tree, our Christmas feast, our mother's unopened gift, our baby dolls, and our father dragged away in handcuffs with the policemen.

The three of us stood in the middle of the room. Sis and I had our arms around our mother's legs. Our mother was standing and sobbing into her hands so hard, her tears were falling onto our hair. The three of us cried for ever so long. We were so sad, helpless, abandoned and confused on our very first Christmas celebration.

Our father returned to the house a few days later. While he was gone our mother just completely lost her mind, again. This breakdown happened very fast with no warning signs. Sis and I stayed away from her the best we could. She would say strange things that made no sense. She would go to the kitchen and throw utensils, dishes, pots and pans all over the floor and against the wall.

She found every candle in the house and there were lots of them. She lit them and set them around the house in every room. She said that God told her things that she should do. She said she was strong and with God's help would do all those things he wanted of her. We were very afraid. This sounded so foreboding. The look in her eye was so evil, so not her. She didn't cry but she laughed. Scary, very scary.

Father took our mother to the hospital. He told us to stay there and do not open the door to anyone. He didn't call anyone to come look after us. We didn't stay with anyone this time—something that had happened only a few times. No friends took care of us, there were none. No family took care of us. We stayed alone in that house and waited for our father to return. Days later he did finally return, without mother.

He told us our mother had to stay at the hospital for a while. That was not something new. What was new was that while mother was in the hospital, father packed up everything that may have belonged to us, probably some things that did not. With all our moves our father had never packed or unpacked anything. A couple days later, with everything loaded in the back of the truck, he drove to the hospital. Sis and I sat quietly next to him.

Sis and I were not permitted in this hospital to visit, but father showed us what window to watch. He told us to stay right next to the truck in this parking lot and watch that specific window that he had pointed out. He went into the hospital and a short time later he was at the window with our mother. Even from where we were in the parking lot, we could see that our mother was in a strange daze just staring straight ahead.

Father took her hand and helped her to wave at us. She just stared straight ahead while her hand was being waved. It was so eerie to see this. Father returned to the truck. He took us to a diner to eat. That night, and for the next several nights, the three of us slept in the truck.

During the next three days father would park the truck at different places and tell us to stay in the truck. He went inside the places and stayed most of the day. We were hungry each day, alone in the truck. He left us in the truck with a "potty bucket." The last day in the truck, he drove us to the Red Cross where we had lunch. As hungry as we were, we could not eat much as our stomachs hurt when we ate.

We stayed at the Red Cross house that whole day. We got to take a bath before bedtime. We slept in a large room with lots of other people. Everyone was doubling up in very small lumpy beds. They all seemed to be families, some with children and both parents. Some children had a mother or a father with them. There were some adults that were just alone.

We were up very early and ate breakfast with all those other families. We had to stand in line for a long time to get our food. My sis and I were all excited to get a little box of cereal. It was a special box that you cut open and pour the milk right into the box. When our father cut open Sandy's cereal box, there were just three tiny pieces of dry cereal in it. Sandy cried.

DESPERATE

Our father said it was a bad box, but the line was too long to stand in again to get another one. Sis cried, not so much because she was so very hungry, but because her cereal box was "broken." I shared my cereal, but it was not enough to stop the hungry feeling. We left the Red Cross building and father drove to the hospital.

Sis and I waited in the parking lot by the truck, looking anxiously at the window. Very soon our father was walking toward the truck leading our mother across the parking lot. There were a couple of hospital people in white clothes following our father. They were both telling him in very loud voices "This is a very bad idea," "She's not ready to leave the hospital yet."

He helped mother into the truck. She was sitting next to father as he drove away. Sis and I were near the passenger door. We could see into the rear-view mirror as we drove from the parking lot. There were several more people there now, all talking very loudly and pointing at the truck and waving their arms in desperation as father drove away.

Mother sat there between us girls and our father. She stared blankly out the front window of the truck. She didn't move at all. She didn't say a word, just stared out the window. We drove for hours in total silence. Sis and I eventually fell asleep.

I awoke a short time later. We were still in the truck. My sis was asleep next to me, her head on my lap. I looked at my parents. Father was driving. It was dark outside now. Mother was sitting just as she was when father first put her in the truck. It was a very eerie sight, my mother. It was like she was sleeping with her eyes open. Staring blankly, not blinking, saying nothing. There are a lot of different kinds of scary, and this was a new one.

Violence

There were people in our lives who thought that my mother made conscious decisions to escape mentally when the world around her was too difficult to face. These were most often her siblings, but they did not live with us. I did wonder about this as I got older. Was this all an act or was she truly so mentally unstable? If this was an act it was a darn good one. Sometimes the "act" lasted for months.

I believed that her daily medications would help her cope with ordinary life situations. Our life was not ordinary, something else I realized as I got older. Living with my parents, even very young, my sis and I became very aware of when our mother was heading toward mental breakdowns.

Some breakdowns were inevitable when she would intentionally stop taking her medications. She did not like taking them. She sometimes felt she didn't need them. Other times, even on medications, they were not strong enough to help her through the abuse she suffered.

Mother would say that the medications numbed her feelings. She could never feel happiness very strongly. She could not feel deep sorrow. She explained that she went through the motions of whatever she had to do, without feeling much of anything.

Perhaps those medications had something to do with why she stayed with my father despite how abusive he was. Perhaps the medications made her numb to the abuse. There were rare occasions that something would happen, and my mother would laugh out loud. It was such a strange sight to see her laugh. It was usually a very bad sign.

My mother would do very strange and sometimes violent things during her breakdowns. She never spoke of God until she started to break down. She would then say that God was directing her to do things and they were not good things. As mentioned, she would set lighted candles up throughout whatever house we happened to be in.

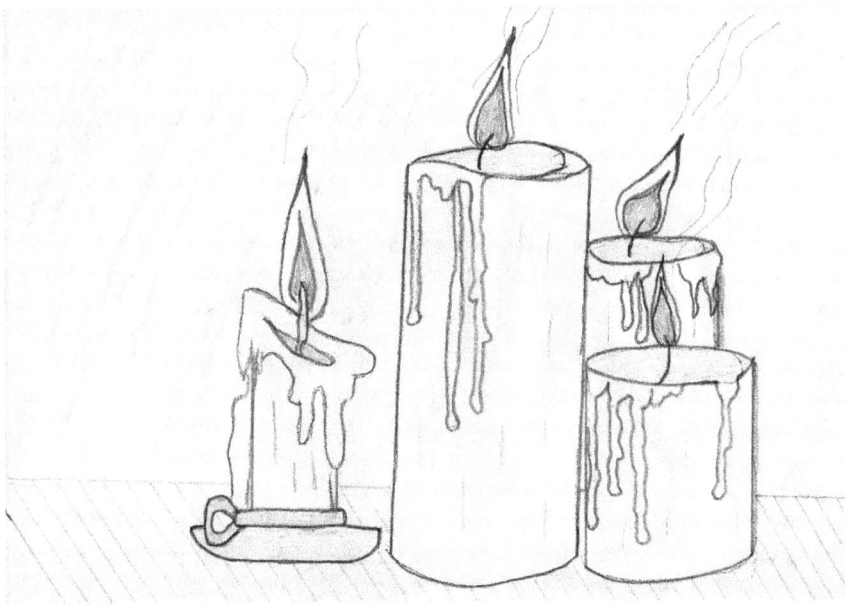

This was often the first sign of trouble, right after the strained laughter. Very scary. Then our mother, a woman who was usually sweet and tender, would become violent. The same abuse she suffered at the hands of our father, she would inflict on my sister and myself. It was at times life-threatening.

She would, of course, rant and rave. She screamed about the power God had given her. She threw garbage out of windows. She refused to dress and went so far as to be outside in her bra and panties. Sis and I were so embarrassed and afraid. We stayed away from her until our father arranged to take her to the hospital.

As time went on, her breakdowns became more violent, maybe because abuse toward her was worse. She would chase my sis and I with various weapons. She once threatened us with a baseball bat. We hid from her in the basement, moving from place to place until our father came home. Our father, whom we feared when he was drunk, would rescue us from our mother when she was crazy.

There was a particularly violent encounter when I was about six. My mother had me go to the basement to find an iron in a box that had been packed away. I found the iron right away, but I dropped it on the concrete floor of the basement and it broke.

I carried the iron up the basement stairs to my mother waiting at the top. I handed the iron to her and told her I had dropped it and it was broken. My mother grabbed the broken iron from my hands, that is the last thing I remember for some time.

My sis told me later that our mother had taken the iron and hit me on the side of the head. I fell down the basement stairs and lay unconscious at the bottom of the stairs on the hard, concrete floor. Mother ran down the stairs and started kicking me. My little sister ran down the stairs also and threw herself on top of me. My five-year-old sister trying to protect me from our violent mother.

Our mother then proceeded to kick my sister. As it turned out, our father happened to come home just when this was happening. He was usually never home in the middle of the day. How fortunate for my sister and I. Sandy said he picked me up, our mother following him, screaming at him and hitting him all the way up the stairs and down the hall to the bedroom.

He laid me in our parents' bed and told Sandy to stay with me. My sis had every intention of staying right by my side, even without our father telling her to. I awoke sometime later. Sandy told me the whole awful story. Sis said she stayed in the bedroom and watched our father through the door try to convince our mother to go to the hospital.

Our mother ran outside, of course, screaming and yelling all about her powers from God. Sandy watched the whole awful scene through the bedroom window. A neighbor called the police. It took several policemen and our father quite a long time to catch our mother. She was running through the neighborhood in her bra and panties. It took four men to forcefully get her into a police car to take her to the hospital.

Through the entire battle to get our mother to the hospital, our father did not even think to mention that he had carried an unconscious daughter to the bedroom. Even with the policemen there, it had not occurred to our father to think of us. Neighbors did not know we even existed.

Sis showed me the many bruises on her body, mostly on her back. They were big and terrible, all purple and orange and puffed out. I swear a couple were actual footprints. I cried for her.

I had a cut on the side of my head, my hair was matted down with dried blood. There were lots of bruises and marks on my body, probably from falling down the stairs. My sis cried for me as she explained that mother had kicked me also. We cried together for a long time. We were convinced that our mother would have killed us if our father had not come home when he did.

After some time, I tried to get out of bed but was so dizzy, I fell backwards onto the big bloody spot I had been lying on. As painful as it was for my little sister to walk, she went to the bathroom and brought a wet washcloth to wipe the blood from my hair. Then there was the blood on the pillowcase to take care of.

When I was finally able to walk, sis and I took the pillowcase to the bathroom and tried to rinse out the blood. We were so afraid of our father being angry for the mess on his bed. How very sad that this was our chief concern.

Our father returned much later that evening. He was drunk and smelled, as usual, of liquor. The cigarette hanging from his bottom lip was not even lit. He never said a word about having left us. He said nothing about our cuts or bruises. He told us not a thing about our mother.

What he did do was try to take my sister down to the basement. We usually never put up a fight when our father ushered either of us to the basement. This night was different. We were already traumatized.

My sister, Sandy, screamed like a banshee, and she wouldn't stop screaming. My father was shocked. Neither my sis nor I had ever done such a thing. When he tried to, again, get her to go down those basement stairs, we both screamed as loudly as we could. He eventually gave up and left us alone.

He left us and went to sit on a chair in the kitchen. He either fell asleep sitting there or he passed out. We could see him from the bedroom. There was that old unlit cigarette dangling from his lip now soaked with drool as the minutes passed. We could smell the liquor even from the distance.

Next morning our father explained that our mother was, again, at the hospital. She would be there for a long time. I was not in school as it was summer. We did not know anyone in this neighborhood as we had not lived here long.

Our father would leave the house every morning. Before he left, he would tell us to stay inside the house. He would say "make sure no one sees you in here. If anyone knows you are in this house, they will take you away. You will never see your mother again."

This may have been the first time we stayed alone while our mother was hospitalized. I'm not sure. We were five and six years old. Of course, we were pretty much alone even when our mother was with us. When our father came home in the evenings, he started packing the few things that had been unpacked. He told us when our mother came home, we were moving. Imagine that!

This was also the first time my sis and I did not visit our mother when she was in the hospital. We were not permitted to visit a mental ward in a hospital, but we always got to wait in the parking lot and wave to our zombie mom. This time, we were simply left alone. At least we had each other.

Our father told us he could not take the chance that the neighbors would see us. He again said we would be taken away and given to strangers if anyone knew we were in the house. Why was this so much more frightening than the way we lived already? Just the same, Sis and I were so careful not to be seen. Despite the inviting sunshine outside, we stayed in the house, alone and together.

We always did take care of each other. We had each other's back. The thought of being taken away and given to strangers was terrifying. What if we were sent to different places? We stayed hidden in that house. There were no toys. We had no television. There was no food,

VIOLENCE

except what our father brought home in the evenings. I don't know how long we did this.

We knew when she finally came home, our mother would not know us. Years later we were told by family, that our mother was given electric shock therapy, not once, but repeatedly. It was a very common treatment for psychiatric patients. It was supposed to calm her by removing any memories of what may have pushed her mind to break. The shock therapy removed so much more of her memory in so many areas.

We moved from the house sis and I had stayed in alone, before our mother even returned to us. Once, my sis and I figured out that we had attended over a dozen different elementary schools as years went by. There was a time we even could recite the names of all the schools.

That means we had moved at least that many times between the ages of six and twelve. With that same math equation, our mother was hospitalized about every year. We never stayed at any school long enough to make friends. We no longer stayed at any house long enough for our parents to meet any neighbors or try to make friends themselves.

When our mother was ready to leave the hospital, my sis and I, for the first time, got to go into the hospital with our father on the day she was released. We probably got to go because it was not in the psych ward. We were in an office. Our father was filling out papers while sis and I sat quietly next to him. We were such good girls.

The person with the papers was telling our father that, "it is very important that you make sure your wife takes her medications. Every time she has a breakdown, each episode will get worse."

We already knew that, we lived through these episodes.

We drove to the next house we would live in. The drive took most of the day. Our mother was sitting in the front seat next to our father. She said not one word, just staring, not seeing, out the front window. We had seen this sight too often.

We were moving far from this area. Our father had packed our few belongings up while our mother was in the hospital. He was getting efficient at packing up our things. Of course, there were not many things to pack. Our mother had no memory of the previous house as we moved into the next. We had simply not been at that previous house long enough.

My sister and I were so familiar with this routine. We would be left with our zombie mother, anxiously waiting for her to remember her daughters. She did always remember how to unpack boxes and set up the next house. I guess that memory was stored in a different area of her fragile brain than the names of her daughters.

It always took a long time, but eventually mother remembered everything. She could recall our names (how nice) and our birthdays. She remembered she was married to our father. She even recalled that she loved him. It was as if the good memories came back to her first. But very soon, she would recall everything. There was a lot of bad to recall. There were more bad memories to recall than good.

When I was older, probably in my teens, I asked my mother if she remembered her violent actions that caused her to be hospitalized. She looked right at me and said through gritted teeth, "I remember everything I ever did and why I did it." For some reason, this statement made me very sad. If she could remember, was she totally unable to control her actions? She couldn't have been even slightly less violent?

Were her siblings correct in thinking that she chose to be a "crazy person" to mentally escape her abusive life? Did she truly remember how violent she was toward her young daughters? I hoped that wasn't true. The violence got worse over the years, just as the doctors had warned.

There was one occasion that she took a knife to her sleeping husband (years after she was divorced from my father) and sliced him across his stomach. He drove himself to the hospital. He told police he was attacked while he walked down the street. He was protecting my mother who could have easily taken his life during one of her violent mental breaks.

Our father never laid an angry hand on us; he saved his brand of drunken violence for our mother. The hand he laid on us was not violent, but the scars he left, though unseen, ran deep in our souls. Our father had been molesting us for years.

He would get me alone and run his hands over my little girl body. He was always drunk and saying sweet things with foul-smelling liquor breath. "You are my sweet soft bunny" or "You are Daddy's precious girl." He would take me somewhere alone, out of sight of my mother or my sister. He always told me that this was our "special secret," and no one should ever know about our special time together.

I know he would take my sister somewhere in the house alone, just as he did me. I knew in my little girl's heart, that he was doing to her the "special secret things" that he did to me. Sis and I never spoke to each other about this, not for many years, even though we knew both of us were going through the same abbusive attention from our father.

I don't know if our mother ever knew. We certainly never told her. We never told anyone. Our father always warned us that we would be separated, so we were totally obedient. We were such good girls, at least that's what our father always told us, alone or together.

Abuse

The touching from my father was happening more and more frequently. He was, as always, drunk when he came home in the evenings. Our mother was, as usual, out of touch with the world. Either too many medications or not enough.

Some evenings he would get only me alone before he would pass out for the night. Other evenings he would first get me alone and then my sister would disappear somewhere in the house with my father. If there happened to be a basement in whatever house we were in, that was father's favorite place to enjoy his secret time with us.

My sister and I were now both in school. I was seven and Sandy was six years old. It is truly amazing how quickly we were signed up for school after we moved to a new community. I didn't know what the process was, but my parents must have had it down to a science.

I did not make friends easily—I had issues. I was shy, quiet and backward. I would literally hide behind my long dark hair. I cried easily at school, over seemingly minor situations. Just teary-eyed and quiet but crying nonetheless. Usually my crying had nothing to do with school. It had everything to do with things I could not talk about, as warned by both my parents.

Some of my teachers were very sweet and patient with the whiny frightened girl I was at school. Never once was I compelled to explain why I was late for school or why I was bruised when I came to school. Of course, if I was ever asked, I would say anything but the truth. I was very conflicted about the things I was experiencing at home, because they did not feel okay.

My sister, on the other hand, made friends very quickly despite her own issues. Sandy was extremely affectionate with her new friends that

ABUSE

she made very fast at school. She was very outgoing and trusting. She took such an interest in every word these kids said. She was easy to like for some, or she was too friendly for others.

This did not bother Sandy in the least. She would latch onto the kids that liked her and would quickly be their best friend. Most of the kids at school lived in our neighborhood. We did get to see them after school when all of us played outside in the evening.

Kids were not permitted to come into whatever house of the month we lived in. We were not permitted in anyone else's home. Although the neighborhood kids would be in and out of each other's homes with friends, sis and I were not permitted to do this. We would be moving soon, I was sure, so friends or no friends, it didn't matter.

In the evenings our life had a routine, like most families I'm sure. Mother was a good cook and would be cooking dinner when we got home from school. We ate together when father arrived home. Unfortunately, he would often get home very late, and always drunk. Our parents would argue.

If the arguing between our parents didn't get terribly bad, we would get to eat. If the arguing became a physical fight, we would go to bed hungry, the food often thrown against the wall. This was something either our father or mother would do out of anger or frustration.

Of course, before we got to go to bed, our father would sneak one of us to the basement while our mother was either washing dishes or cleaning food off the walls. The secret encounters were happening more often, and they were becoming intense and rough.

Whereas our father used to touch me on top of my clothing, he was now touching me beneath my clothes. There was no more sweet talk and he was squeezing and pinching to the point in which I would bruise and cry. I tried to avoid these secret encounters, but on the other hand, if he cornered me, I would obediently go to the basement with him.

Something more heartbreaking than these encounters was happening within the walls of our home. My sister, Sandy, and I were very quiet when we were alone together. We no longer shared everything that we were going through. Of course, our father warned us always to not share these encounters.

Although we did not talk about these awful secrets, I knew my sister was going through them also. I wondered what she thought about these secrets. I wondered if our father was rough with her also. Years later we talked about the abuse. More than the abuse, we were sorry we stopped sharing our pain. We were so afraid to disobey our father.

Then there was a big change in our lives. We moved to another house that not only had a basement, sis and I had our own room. We shared a room together and we were no longer in the room with our parents. We each had our own little bed. That crib we had shared for so many years was finally gone. Funny thing about this new set up, we would sleep together in one bed.

Our father started to come to our room after we went to bed to, "say good night." He would find us together in one bed and scold us saying, "I got you each a bed and expect you to sleep in them. I don't want to ever check on you at night and find you sleeping together." Of course, we obeyed our father. We were such good girls.

As it turned out, there was quite a different reason he wanted us in separate beds. He would sneak into our bedroom late at night and get one of us up to take to the basement. So many times, I pretended to be asleep when he sneaked in. He would simply take my sister from the room. How sad was that?

I am very sure that on just as many nights, when he came and got me out of my bed, my sister was pretending to be asleep in hers. Sis and I never spoke of these occasions, until we were much older. Even then, we did not tell our mother what was happening to us as she was always either heading toward a breakdown or emerging from one.

Sis and I now had bruises that were not a result of our mother slapping or hitting us. We had bruises from our father who was very rough with us when he got us alone. We had blue and purple marks on us where he would pinch so hard. The marks were not where anyone could see, except our mother who would get us ready for our baths.

We were bathed together, don't know why. Perhaps it was to save time. There were many times mother asked one or the other of us where we got the marks and bruises. We always shrugged our shoulders and said we didn't know.

She would yell, "If I find out you're hurting each other I will give you both a beating." This was a shocking statement coming from our mother who often physically hurt us. Eventually she just stopped asking about our many bruises.

I never for a second thought of telling my mother where the bruises and marks came from. Obviously, neither did Sandy. I did wonder, years later, if our mother had the slightest inkling about what was going on. Did she know what our father was doing? Perhaps she had an idea but was just as afraid to ask us as we were afraid to tell her.

One evening something happened that changed everything. Father came home from work with two men. They were friends of our father from work. They had dinner with us and went on and on about what a wonderful cook our mother was. Mother was tickled. Our father seemed a bit aggravated with the attention Mother was getting.

After dinner, the men and father were in the front-room listening to a football game on the radio. They were drinking and smoking cigarettes nonstop. They were sure carrying on and getting louder and louder. Our mother was busy in the kitchen cleaning up, as there was more than usual to clean.

Sis and I were in our bedroom, trying to get away from the noise and thick cigarette smoke. Our father came into our room and took me by the hand and said to Sandy, "Be quiet." He took me down the stairs drunk and stumbling, while those two men, strangers in our home, were still listening to the football game. Some things you just try to block out, although I always remembered more than I wish I had. I always remembered that rancid odor of stale cigarettes and foul liquor breath and the strange men in our house yelling loudly about the game on the radio . . . and being in the basement that particular night.

A streetlight was shining through a basement window. My father stood me on a stool where the light was shining through. He had his hands under my clothing pinching and squeezing me so hard. Tears were streaming down my face, but I did not cry out. Suddenly the pain between my thighs and on my little girl parts was terrible.

My father quickly picked me up and carried me to the other side of the basement. He sat me down on the floor and left me there. He stumbled up the basement stairs. I could hear the two men yelling excitedly and whooping at the radio, still listening to that game. I could hear mother busy in the kitchen doing something. I could hear someone crying, it was me.

I was sitting on the basement floor holding my hand between my thighs against my body. I was hurting so much. I felt something fall into my hand. It was dark where I was sitting, so I closed my fist to keep hold of what had fallen into my hand and walked toward the window and into the light shining through the window. I opened my hand to look.

I stopped suddenly when I realized that my father was by that same window and had my little sis standing on the same stool that he had put me on. I could see them so clearly in the light shining through the basement window. I started to cry again very quietly. He was hurting my sister; I knew he was.

I glanced down at my hand and there in my palm were three pennies, and a small amount of blood. Is this what had hurt me so much? Suddenly I heard my sister cry out. I heard my drunken father tell her to be very quiet, so, she cried very quietly. I ran up those basement stairs to my bed and cried very loudly into my pillow.

Very soon my sister came into the room. She climbed into my bed with me. Neither of us said a word. We held onto each other and both cried very quietly, but we still said nothing. We were startled when our mother came into the room to announce that she was getting a bath ready for us.

We went to the bathroom for our bath. We could hear our father and the two men still yelling with excitement over the football game. They were still drinking, I'm sure. Mother rolled her eyes at their loud yelling. Sis and I both took off our clothes and stepped into the tub. The warm water felt so good.

ABUSE

As mother always did, she splashed us with the warm water while we were standing in the tub. She then soaped us up good and then we sat in the water to rinse off. Sometimes we even got to play in the water for a while. We did not care to play tonight.

As mother was soaping Sandy up on the inside of her legs, she noticed blood on the inside of my little sister's thigh. Mother looked closer. She was cleaning Sandy gently between her legs when a penny suddenly appeared in mother's hand. Sandy started to cry.

She was crying rather quietly but shaking hard. Sandy was trembling head to toe. I started to tremble also. We could not stop shaking and we were not even cold. My first thought was, "Oh no, please no, no, no. Don't let this be happening." Our father will be so angry.

Our mother looked at the penny in her hand. She was shocked. She said, "Sandy what did you do?" "Did you put this penny inside yourself?" Sandy just kept crying. Mother gently continued to wash my little sister. Two more pennies fell into mother's hand mixed with blood.

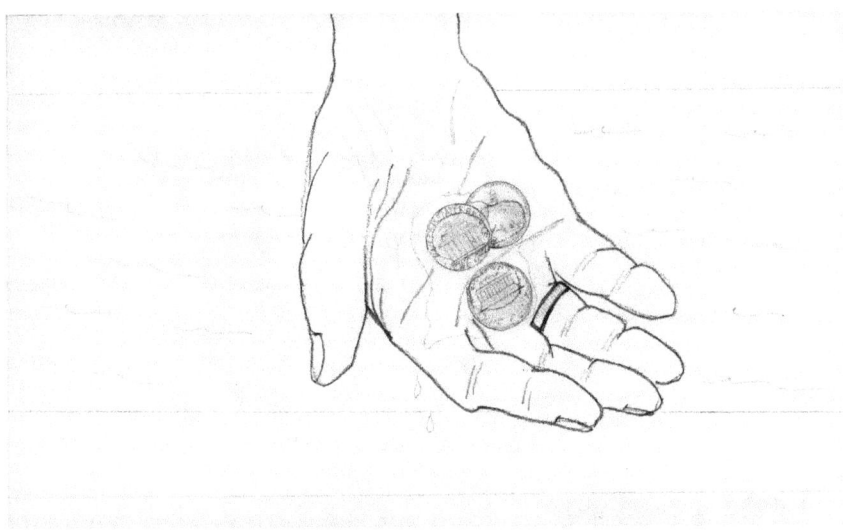

My mother gasped and frantically yelled, "Did one of those strange men hurt you; did they do this to you, Sandy?"

My little sister screamed out through her tears "Those are my daddy's pennies; he gave them to me in the basement." Mother stared at Sandy in shocked disbelief. She looked toward me; of course, I was crying.

My mother was stunned and horrified at what her daughter had said. My little sister cried, "My daddy put the pennies inside of me at our secret place." My mother stared at my sister. My mother looked at the bloody pennies in the palm of her hand. Tears welled up in my mother's eyes. She dropped those pennies into the tub and rinsed her hand of the blood.

She turned to look at me, now standing there shivering in the tub next to my sister. I was still crying along with my sister. My one hand was in a tight fist. I had not even been aware of it. I had not even noticed this when I undressed for my bath. My mother took my tight-fisted hand in hers and uncurled my fingers. There were three bloody pennies in my palm.

My mother gasped in horror. Then she did something she had never done before. She put her arms around my little sis and me and cried. She cried a long time and kept saying, "I am so sorry, I'm so very sorry. I love you girls. I love you so much." Soon we were all crying. Sis and I standing naked in the tub with our mother's arms around us, all of us crying together.

We heard the front door open and then close. Mother told us to dry off. She said' "Get dressed, I will be right back." She left the bathroom for just a few minutes. She returned quickly and said, "Your father and his friends have left. I don't want you girls to be afraid. I am calling the police to come and get us before your father comes back to the house."

Mother called the police right then and there. We dried ourselves off in the bathroom and got dressed in our pajamas. We could not hear what she was saying as she was in another room, but we knew she was on the phone for quite some time.

A few minutes later we heard our father's truck approaching the house. That old beat up truck had a very distinctive squeaking and noisy sound to it. At the very same time that we heard the truck, we saw a police car pulling into the driveway.

ABUSE

Sis and I were watching out the window. Mother was nervously pacing back and forth in the front room. She was wringing her hands, biting her lip, and fighting back tears. "Girls, please get away from that window," she pleaded.

I could see the red taillights of my father's truck disappearing down the street. I remember thinking, this is where our family gets separated. Finally, it was just the dim streetlights shining on the empty pavement and lighting up the police car in the driveway.

Mother talked to the policemen for quite a while. She explained about bathing sis and me. She told the policemen about the pennies she had found on us and what my little sister had said. She explained to the policemen that she had thought one of the strange men had hurt us. She kept repeating, "I would have never thought George would hurt our daughters; he loved them so."

Mother was very calm. She did not cry. She looked so strong and brave sitting there speaking with the two policemen. "I have been through so much with my husband for years," mother said, not going into detail. The two policemen both seemed very shaken by her story. They answered, "We're so very sorry, ma'am." Mother told us to answer the policemen's questions. We were both so afraid.

The policemen were very careful with us and kind to us. My sis and I answered the questions we were asked. We ended up telling so much and it was so easy. The first time our mother truly reacted was when she realized how long we had been molested by our father. She really had no idea!? Tears fell down her cheeks and then she was sobbing into her hands.

The policemen never asked a single question about our mother. They had no knowledge of her own kind of abuse. What did it matter now, considering the trauma we had suffered this evening? The policemen insisted that they drive us to the hospital. They said, "It's a very good idea to have a doctor check your daughters out."

At the hospital they tried to separate us, and we were both, for the first time, immediately hysterical. A decision was quickly made to keep us together. Our mother sat some distance away, but she was in the room with us. She could hear our answers to their questions and cried about what she heard. We both explained about the bruises, trips to the basement, and threats to not talk of these encounters. Nurses, doctors and our mother were all very upset.

Everyone was so kind to my sister and me. At the hospital the doctors and nurses checked us over from head to toe. They asked us lots of questions that we both answered quickly. Why did it feel so good to talk about these "secrets" that we had kept to ourselves for so long? We had been threatened to not ever tell anyone and we were telling everyone.

As careful as they were with us, the check-ups were uncomfortable and embarrassing. One of the doctors explained to our mother that "there was no deep vaginal trauma, only superficial scrapes and scratches." Sis and I did not understand. Mother cried but seemed relieved at the same time.

After our "check-ups" a very nice lady drove us back to the house. The lady kept a light and happy conversation going with our mother. Every time the lady glanced our way, a sad look came over her face. When we pulled into the driveway at the house, we stayed in the car with the lady. Mother went in the house "to pack a few things to take with us."

Our mother packed a suitcase with some clothing. There was no sign of father. The lady then drove us to a Red Cross center where we were to spend the night. One of our mother's siblings, an uncle we had never met, was coming to get us first thing in the morning.

The Runaways

Sis and I had stayed at a different Red Cross center previously. At that time, we were with our father and our mother was in the hospital. This time, we were with our mother and our father was just gone. We were a family separated, just like father and even our mother had always warned.

We slept that night, all three of us in one bed. We were assigned two beds but chose to sleep together in one. Sis and I slept wonderfully, but our mother did not sleep at all. When we woke up, we enjoyed a very nice breakfast with the other families. This was a much better breakfast than at the other Red Cross center.

While we were still eating, a strange-looking man walked into the dining room. The image of the man was startling. The chatter from all the families stopped. Everyone in the dining room turned to gawk and stare at this intruder. You could not help but notice him; he was quite a colorful character.

He was dressed differently from any man in the dining room—different than anyone I had ever seen. He wore blue jeans with the legs tucked into tall, shiny green scaly-looking cowboy boots. Those boots had thick heels and were very noisy when he walked into the dining room.

He wore a red t-shirt tucked into his jeans. Around his waist was a wide, black leather belt with a huge silver belt buckle that had "Harley" embossed on it. He wore a black leather vest with lots of long black fringe hanging down. He wore big dark sunglasses with bright yellow frames.

A red, white and blue bandana was tied around his head holding back very long, greasy and wavy hair. He had a beard and mustache.

He held a blue cap in his hands that had "Cleveland Indians" in red lettering on it. He had lots of chains hanging off the big black belt and tucked into a pocket of his jeans. He spotted our mother and smiled ear to ear. He seemed genuinely tickled to see her. Two of his front teeth were shiny silver.

Mother told us to finish eating our breakfast; yum, it was good. Mother literally ran to the man and threw her arms around his neck. He hugged her tight and picked her right off the floor. She looked so tiny and childlike with him. She was crying and that big man was teary-eyed. She spoke with him for a very long time.

Sis and I were sure the man must be the uncle we had been told would come get us. I don't know what we'd expected, but this man was not it. He was not an especially big man, but his presence, looks and character filled the room. Eventually, the other families stopped staring and went back to enjoying their breakfast.

Mother came to the table with the strange man in tow, holding his hand as she pulled him across the room. He had a very nervous expression on his face as we were introduced to him. Although he looked nervous, he had very beautiful and kind eyes. He had our mother's eyes.

He knelt in front of us and explained very gently that he was going to drive us to our grandparents' farm in West Virginia. Really! How wonderful! We loved our grandparents and their beautiful farm.

We were suddenly so excited, even happy. We had visited our grandparents a couple times in the past and we loved them and the farm so much. West Virginia was so beautiful with trees, mountains and rivers. Both our parents had been born in West Virginia, as had I.

A man walked up to our uncle and invited him to have some breakfast. The four of us finished a very tasty breakfast. Our uncle was very hungry. He explained that he had left to come get us as soon as he was told we needed his help. He drove straight through the night from Florida to get here and had not eaten in two days.

Our uncle was a long-haul trucker. As if our uncle himself had not been enough of a shock, when we walked outside, his huge semi-truck was waiting for us. It was the cab part of the truck with no trailer attached. That cab was huge even without the trailer; it was as big as a small house. What a wonderful way to get to our grandparents' farm.

He had to give mother a boost to get her up into that cab. He picked up Sandy and then me and handed each of us to our mother. As the three of us were getting situated, we had yet another surprise. There was a dog in the truck. That little dog was certainly telling us off. He was as shocked to see us as we were to see him.

Our uncle pulled himself into the truck cab behind the steering wheel. "You behave now, Pedro," our uncle said sternly. Pedro was very small with long wispy hair that was particularly long on his tail and over his eyes. His hair was black, white and brown in a random pattern. He was a very pretty, little dog. Sandy and I squealed with delight, much to the shock of the little dog.

Pedro jumped into a large compartment behind the front seat. My uncle explained that this was the sleeper compartment. He also explained that Pedro was not accustomed to being around children and he certainly never had to share his truck with anyone. "Pedro is a good dog. He may pout at you, but he would never hurt anyone."

GLIMPSES OF HELL

As we pulled away and were driving down the street, people were pointing at the huge cab. They were stopping and staring as we drove by. It did look out of place on the little side streets. Kids were waving and making a pulling gesture with their arms and hands. Our uncle would pull a chain above his head and a very loud horn would sound. The kids on the street as well as sis and I were thrilled.

The four of us were sitting in the front seat, except Pedro, who had decided to stay in the sleeping compartment behind us. The little dog had his back toward us, because he was pouting as our uncle had said he would. When our uncle would talk to Pedro, he would wag his tail, but he would not turn his head around or look in our direction.

Pedro was a very intelligent little dog, according to our uncle. He was a tiny chihuahua with a very big attitude. He'd traveled with our uncle on every long-haul trip since our uncle found him five years earlier, a tiny puppy thrown into a dumpster at a truck stop. The pup was wet, dirty and near death. My uncle had nursed him back to health and they had become inseparable.

Pedro was very jealous when anyone else got some of our uncle's attention, but he was sweet, and we were told he would never bite anyone. Our uncle invited us to sleep in the compartment if we were tired. He assured us that the little dog might be annoyed, but he was perfectly safe to be around.

Sandy and I were wide awake and so excited. We were enjoying this adventure. We were not even thinking about our father or our terrible evening with him, the police, the hospital and the Red Cross center. Everything around us seemed bright and happy, new and exciting.

Our mother sat next to her brother. The two of them were talking non-stop, and based on the conversation, had a lot of catching up to do. After a while, our mother who had not slept at all the night before, fell asleep with her head resting against her brother's shoulder.

As if our morning had not had enough surprises already, our uncle started singing, very quietly. He was singing gospel hymns. Now if you could see the man, you would have been shocked—he did not look the part. He then sang some rather nice country songs.

THE RUNAWAYS

He had a very deep, soothing voice. Sis and I were enjoying this so much. He would glance over at my sister and me occasionally, looking at us with our mother's beautiful eyes. When he smiled, those silver teeth shone.

Sandy and I sat next to the opposite window, hand in hand. We were watching out the window and looking at everything as we drove past. We were talking and giggling and enjoying each other more than we had in a very long time. I had been missing my sister and was not even aware of how much, until just now. What a strange thing to think of.

For a very quick second I thought of my father. Father was a handsome man. He was always very well dressed and clean cut. He was very charming, and people liked him, just to look at him. Father did not look scary at all, but father was very scary. Father was the stuff of nightmares to little girls.

Here was our uncle. Everything about our uncle was scary, until you looked in his eyes. Sis and I felt safe and happy with this very scary looking long-haul trucker. As years went by and we came to know the man better, we came to love and trust him like very few people in our lives. He would come to the rescue of my sis and I and our mother many more times in the future.

As it turned out, we were at a house in Cleveland, Ohio, when father molested us this last time. It was Cleveland police that came to the house and doctors at a Cleveland hospital that examined us. It was at a Red Cross center on the east side of Cleveland that we spent the night and enjoyed the nice breakfast.

Our uncle lived in Cleveland, but he was doing a long-haul transport to Florida when he received a call about us. He was told by a dispatcher through his company, where to find us. He had driven over twelve hours straight through from Florida to Ohio to pick us up. Now he was driving the eight hours from Ohio to where our grandparents' farm was in West Virginia.

You would have thought our uncle would be the one nodding off to sleep. He told our mother before she dozed off not to worry; he was used to staying awake for days at a time. He said he made better money that way. He also said, "I have these little miracle pills that keep me awake." He opened a small bottle and popped a handful of white pills into his mouth.

So, we were on the run, so to speak. Heading cross-country in this giant semi-truck cab with our scary looking uncle and his beautiful little dog. When mother awoke a short time later, she began talking with our uncle about the Cleveland police. She was explaining how kind and patient they had been when they talked to the three of us at length.

They'd driven us to the hospital and then waited to hear what the doctor found. They told our mother that they would find our father and have him arrested. They explained to mother that once they found father, they wanted her to testify against him in court.

The police had wanted mother to stay in Cleveland to see this through. Mother was afraid to stay. She was afraid of what our father was very capable of doing, so she got in touch with her brother. Sis and I heard her mentioning that she was fearful our father would show up at the farm. He would know that was where she'd go.

Our uncle laughed. "He'd be a total fool to come looking for you, sis. Every person in our family is a dead aim with a rifle, and he knows that. You'll be perfectly safe. Mom and dad are going to be as tickled as I was to see you and these babies."

Sandy and I did eventually fall asleep, to the sound of our mother laughing with her brother over his stories. Not only could he sing, he was also very funny. He seemed to enjoy hearing his sister's laugh and was determined to take her mind off the hurtful things the three of us had been through. We woke up when suddenly the truck was bumping and bouncing so much that it shook the entire cab.

Our uncle was driving that huge cab right up the dirt road to our grandparents' farm. It couldn't even fit on the road, but he fearlessly or foolishly kept on going. Sis and I stopped looking out the side window, because we knew those huge tires were hanging over the edge. Sis and I were not the least bit afraid; we were just excited and so happy.

THE RUNAWAYS

Our uncle said he would drive as far as he could and then we would have to walk. Mother mentioned that he would never be able to turn this cab around and uncle said, "I'll just back it down the road, sis. No worries."

Our mothers' eyes were as wide as our own. Our uncle looked at the three of us and just laughed.

Soon, the cab could go no further. Our uncle stopped it dead in the road. We had to walk the rest of the way. As soon as he opened the cab door, little Pedro jumped out onto the dirt road. That little dog was running in happy circles, barking excitedly and wagging his tail. He had a silly dog smile on his little face. He was so glad to be out of the truck.

It was just turning dusk, but it was a beautiful evening. As we started to walk, our uncle picked up my little sis and put her on his shoulders. She squealed with excitement. Pedro had a pouty expression on his doggy face for just a second, and then charged joyfully ahead. "When you get tired, Brenda, I'll carry you for a while." I didn't get tired for the entire walk. I was too excited.

Our uncle started singing again. He was singing those gospel hymns. Much to our surprise, our mother was singing along with him. We did not know she even knew these songs. Sis and I were enjoying this part of our trip as much as we enjoyed the ride to West Virginia in the big truck.

We came to a spot in the road where there was suddenly a trail that led sharply downhill. This was a two-mile trail that would take us to the farm. Sis and I asked if we could run ahead. Our mother said yes, so we held hands and were laughing and skipping ahead of the adults.

I did not feel like we were the same girls that lived in Cleveland yesterday. My little sister was laughing with me and our mother was laughing with her brother. The horrible incidents of yesterday seemed very far away. Suddenly a great fear came over me, something bad was sure to happen to ruin this happy time, as it always did. Thank goodness the sense of foreboding passed quickly.

We came to the bottom of the trail. To the right, across a beautiful meadow and a crystal-clear river, up a small hill and through a white picket fence with a trellis covered in bright red roses, was our grandparents' farmhouse. Our uncle hugged our mother, "Welcome home, sis," he said. Mother was crying.

Sandy and I continued to run ahead. We ran through the meadow, across the bridge over the bubbling river and up the hill to the farmhouse. Our grandmother was on the porch and when we ran up the stairs, she scooped us both into her arms for a big, happy hug. This entire day felt like a wonderful dream from which I did not want to awaken.

Grandpa was in the house waiting. When we walked into the house, the first thing he did was hug our mother saying, "We're so relieved that you're here." He then knelt in front of us and hugged my little sis and me. My grandpa was usually a quiet and reserved man, not openly affectionate. Sis and I were so happy and surprised with his special greeting.

Grandma had warmed up some food for us. It was the very best chicken and biscuits I had ever eaten. After we ate, our mother tucked sis and me into one of the big brass beds in our grandparents' room. "Please try to get some sleep, girls, I'll be in later."

We heard the adults talking although we could not hear what was being said. We recognized each of their voices. They talked long into the night. Sandy and I could not fall asleep; we had so much to talk about ourselves. We lay in the cozy, comfy bed holding hands and whispered to each other. We did not talk about anything sad or scary. We talked about our wonderful day.

Our grandmother came into the room to kiss us good night. When she found us awake, she decided to tell us a story. She told us about a little boy whose parents would always fight and argue. They were also very hurtful to the little boy, always hitting him and screaming bad things at him. He was just a little boy, alone.

She said that the parents became more and more violent until one evening something very terrible happened. The little boy was hiding behind the couch. He always hid when his mother and father fought.

In the middle of this fight between his parents the little boy's very angry father took a gun and shot his wife and then himself.

When the police came to the house and found this terrible scene, they also found the little boy. He was sitting quietly behind the couch. The policemen arranged to take the little boy to a home for abandoned children, as he had no other family. The people there were very caring and loving.

One day all the children being cared for at the home were walking down the hall with teachers to their classes. The little boy, new to the classes, stopped in front of a painting in the hall. He was very excited, crying and laughing and talking at the same time. Pointing to the painting he said, "That is the kind man that was with me every time my parents would fight. He was always with me wherever I hid." This is the first time the little boy had spoken since he was brought to the home. "I know him, that kind man was always with me," said the little boy.

His teacher went to him and hugged him. She was so thrilled that he was speaking. This was a big breakthrough for the little homeless boy. She was still kneeling by his side as she glanced at the painting that he was so excited about. Her eyes filled with tears. Her heart was full.

This was a beautiful painting of Jesus sitting among many little children. Grandma told us that below the painting was written "Let the little children come to me." My sister and I did not know much about Jesus, but for some reason, despite the sad content, we both liked our grandma's story. We could relate to the little boy, although his story was far worse.

That little boy, although he had no sister or brother, was not alone through those awful times. The "kind man," Jesus, had always been with him. Sandy and I always had each other. As years went by, sis and I would be spending much more time with our grandparents. We would be learning so much more about Jesus and his love from our patient and loving grandmother.

Right now, it was wonderful to feel safe and loved. We were in a very different world, if only for a little while. We don't know why our grandma shared that story, but we both liked it. As sad as the little boy's young life was, there was joy at the end of the story and there was hope. Perhaps there was hope for my little sis and our mother and me. Perhaps there could be joy.

Tales of Marriages and Hospitals

Melbalene did not return to Cleveland to see things through as the police wanted her to. She stayed with her daughters on the farm. To see them happy and laughing filled her heart. Although there were still a couple weeks left in the school year, she chose not to enroll them at school in West Virginia.

Melbalene did get a divorce from George. She made a couple quick trips to Cleveland with her brother to take care of that. While she was gone, Brenda and Sandy stayed on the farm. Melbalene knew they would be completely safe and happy here with their grandparents, like never before in their young lives.

Melbalene didn't even realize just how unhappy she and her daughters really were until suddenly they were safe and happy. Melbalene tried not to think of George. She and her girls were very much loved by her parents. There was no screaming or fighting. There was no hitting or hiding. There were hugs, encouragement, love and trust.

The girls were given little chores to do every day. They would sweep the floors, gather the eggs or feed the chickens. They were so tickled to help their grandparents. Melbalene was so proud of her young daughters. After their chores the girls played most of the remainder of the day, usually outdoors. They seemed to always find ways to play together and keep each other entertained. Her girls were truly close. You could easily tell that they had genuine love and concern for one another.

Melbalene helped her mother take care of the house and do chores. She helped cook the meals every day. The biggest meal of the day was breakfast. She wanted to help however she could. Both ladies were good cooks and they enjoyed being together. They would sing the gospel songs her brother had sung on their drive to West Virginia in his truck. Melbalene and her girls were safe here.

Through the entire time they were running away from Cleveland and settling in West Virginia, Melbalene did very well. She did not feel unstable or emotional. She did not fall apart. She felt strong in the fact that she did what she had to do to save her daughters from their father. She tried not to dwell on the nightmare events.

She was determined to stay strong. She was still shocked at what George had been doing to their daughters. She was ashamed that she had been unaware of the abuse Brenda and Sandy had endured for so long. She was heartbroken that, probably for many reasons, her daughters had not come to her. She was trying not to think of George. Of course, she thought of him every day. There was a time Melbalene thought they would be together forever.

Melbalene decided she would be careful to take her medications, though she hated taking them because they kept her in a fog. However, she also wondered if maybe if she was not medicated, she would have been aware that something was wrong with George and their girls. Maybe she shouldn't take those medications as they dimmed her feelings. She was, as always, conflicted about these medications.

TALES OF MARRIAGES AND HOSPITALS

Melbalene was happier than she had been for a very long time. She found herself laughing and singing. It helped that her parents were so supportive. They never once said a word to make her feel ashamed of her circumstances. They made her and her daughters feel so loved, so safe and so welcomed.

In some ways, Melbalene was alone without her husband. She had always wanted her own loving family. She was now a young divorced woman not yet thirty years old. Her beautiful daughters were ages six and seven, just a year apart. Would she ever have her own loving family?

Melbalene was not alone long. She was only divorced a couple of months when, to the concern and amazement of her parents, she remarried! Her new husband was the twin brother of a young Baptist pastor from a church in Webster Springs. The girls noticed the young man on the farm often but did not really pay attention as they were happily enjoying their own new adventure.

While her daughters were so busy adjusting to and enjoying life on the farm, Melbalene had become involved with this young man. She was thrilled with the attention. The young man was at the farm almost every day. He was very quiet and polite. He didn't drink or smoke. He prayed a lot. Her parents also liked him, but this was too soon, and he was so young.

He was a handsome young man and very attentive toward Melbalene. His name was Quinton. He visited the farm almost every day after work and on weekends. He was sweet with her girls. He had come to love the beautiful Melbalene very much and very quickly. Just months after they met he asked her to marry him. He did not want this beautiful woman to get away.

Just as fast, his brother, the pastor, had the marriage dissolved. Quinton was forbidden from ever seeing Melbalene again. The sad part was that, for whatever reason, Quinton went along with his brother's unreasonable demands. It seems the entire "religious" family of the young preacher and his twin brother was against this "very fast surprise marriage."

The pastor said, "This divorced woman is of loose moral values and mentally unstable." Melbalene was heart-broken but her mother said "Melbalene, you have to slow down." After the marriage was dissolved, Melbalene became very depressed very quickly, which was always very scary.

Melbalene's father drove her to visit a doctor in town as soon as he noticed her change in behavior. She came home with her father the same day. Everyone was surprised that there was no hospital stay needed. Her father had insisted that she get help quickly. That fact probably made all the difference, especially since Melbalene was more than willing to get help. She seemed better, not as depressed, even happy again.

A visit from the brother who had driven her little family to West Virginia cheered her up even more. He had some very good news. It seems that one of their sisters was also divorced and living in Cleveland. Her sister sent word that if Melbalene would move in with her at her apartment in Cleveland, her sister could get Melbalene a job.

After discussion with her parents, it was decided that she would return to Cleveland. She would settle in with her sister and hopefully start a new job. She would than arrange for Brenda and Sandy to join her in Cleveland. The idea of returning to Cleveland made Melbalene a little bit nervous, but it was a big city and nowhere near the area that she and George had stayed.

Her girls got to stay with their grandparents on the farm while their mother settled into this new life in Cleveland. It was difficult to tell who was happier, the girls or their grandparents. The grandparents were both excited to get to know the girls. Also, after what they'd been through, the girls needed to feel safe and loved.

Melbalene was anxious about leaving her young daughters. This was the first time her girls would be away from her for such a long time. Melbalene knew that this was the right thing to do, but it was not easy for her.

This was also the first of many summers Brenda and Sandy would stay on their grandparents' farm for an entire summer. Here, they were comfortable being away from their mother. They did not mention their father, not even to each other. There was always the chance that the mere mention of him would cause something bad to happen. Brenda and Sandy were so happy, so content, so no reason to tempt fate.

That beautiful farm in West Virginia was the best place on earth for the girls to heal from their unspeakable trauma. They seemed to have put any unsettling thoughts or memories right out of their minds. They shared every adventure on the farm with joy and genuine excitement. The girls were very sweet and polite to their grandparents. They were good girls that cared very much for each other and everything around them.

In Cleveland, Melbalene was very busy settling into her new life. She really did get a job working in a factory with her sister. Her very first job, ever. She was so excited about this. They worked different shifts during the week so were not often home together. The sisters were off work on weekends.

They were young divorced women and enjoyed going out to meet people, especially young men.

Melbalene was a beautiful woman and her sister was very pretty, also. The sisters did get a lot of attention when they were out and about. Very soon, both Melbalene and her sister met some young men at their workplace and were dating them.

The newest young man in Melbalene's life was Vaughn. He started dating Melbalene while her young daughters were staying at the farm. They were still dating when the girls moved back to Cleveland. The girls moved in with their mother, Melbalene, and her sister (their aunt). They missed the farm but were happy to be with their mother again.

Melbalene was very happy. She had a job and was taking care of her girls. She got along so well with her sister. They were close and such good friends. Her sister liked Vaughn and approved of Melbalene dating, even if it happened so quickly. Brenda and Sandy also liked Vaughn. Melbalene again dreamed of having "her own family, a good family."

Vaughn was nice and he was funny. He was a wonderful cook—the first man Melbalene ever knew that could cook so well. It was a nice surprise. He enjoyed cooking fancy meals, packing everything up and taking all of them on picnics. They were like a real family when they were all together.

Melbalene really liked her new job and her new-found freedom. The girls stayed with their aunt when their mother worked the day shifts. They were with their mother in the evenings (which is when Melbalene's sister worked). It worked out well for everyone. It was a nice arrangement. Melbalene was doing very well—still very focused on "having her own family" though.

Sadly, the nice arrangement did not last long. Melbalene's sister was soon pregnant and planning to marry the young man she had been seeing. When the sister moved out of the apartment, Melbalene announced that she and Vaughn were also getting married and said, "We can be a family, a happy family." This meant so much to Melbalene.

They were married. Vaughn moved into the apartment. He insisted Melbalene give up her job as he was the man and would care for the family. For a short time, everything was wonderful, and they were a "happy family." Then something bad started to happen. It was a familiar kind of bad. Vaughn was not coming home until late and when he did, the smell of liquor came home with him. Melbalene was heartbroken and her daughters were scared.

Melbalene and Vaughn started arguing. It seems Vaughn was drinking more than he was paying the bills. Melbalene became deeply depressed and started acting unusually strange. Something Vaughn had never seen before and didn't know about. The girls had seen this strange behavior many times. Brenda and Sandy were again hiding.

But there was something new in their mother's behavior they had not seen before. Melbalene became extremely violent with Vaughn. This was not something she'd done in the past. She was now the aggressor. Vaughn had to call the police for help. He told them his wife was dangerous to herself and others, even her own daughters. He was, unfortunately, right to say that.

When the police were able to subdue her, Melbalene was taken to

TALES OF MARRIAGES AND HOSPITALS

the hospital. Brenda and Sandy saw the entire terrible struggle between the police and Melbalene. Their mother was taken away in a white jacket that wrapped around her and forced her arms to her sides. This was a new type of trauma for the young girls and Melbalene.

The girls stayed with their now pregnant aunt and her new husband while their mother was in the hospital. Their aunt loved them but was very impatient and strict with them. The girls did not like the husband, there was something strangely familiar and scary about him. He was a drinker, perhaps that was why they were scared. They longed to be with their grandparents. They missed their mother.

Shortly after Melbalene was released from the hospital she returned to the apartment that she and Vaughn shared with the girls. Vaughn had taken all his belongings and had left for good. Melbalene did not want to deal with another alcoholic, but it was Vaughn that started the divorce process. The last thing Vaughn said to her was "I don't want a crazy woman for my wife."

Melbalene had given up her job at Vaughn's insistence after they married. She could not pay for the apartment. She had no income and could pay for nothing. She and the girls moved in with her sister and her new husband. This was a very sad turn of events. The girls were happy to find out that she was making plans to return to the farm. Then suddenly, those plans were changed.

A lady friend of Melbalene's from the factory called her. She and her husband were moving to Illinois. Melbalene and this lady had become close while working together in the factory. The friend insisted that Melbalene and her daughters come to Illinois with them. They could stay with her and her husband until Melbalene found a job in Illinois.

Melbalene said yes to this very strange idea. Brenda and Sandy were shocked at the whole thing. They had met the couple and liked the friend and her husband, but they wanted to return to West Virginia, not move to Illinois. However, they did move to Illinois, as they had no choice. Their mother could "start another whole new life", as she said. She could "maybe find myself as I don't know who I am."

Brenda and Sandy shared a tiny bedroom with their mother in a small cramped apartment in Illinois. The couple were very kind to the little family, but it was difficult. The tiny cramped rooms were in a big apartment building, surrounded by so many other big apartment buildings.

There was no yard to play in. There were no trees or grass or sunshine to enjoy. To make matters worse, Melbalene did not do well finding a job. She was distraught and depressed. Her friends were concerned as they were very aware of her history of mental breakdowns.

One day a letter came to Melbalene in care of her friend's address in Illinois. It was from a man she had met when she and her sister went out on weekends from their factory job. The man said in the letter he could not stop thinking of her.

He wrote in his letter that he had run into Vaughn and found out they were divorced. He explained in his letter that it took him a long time to track her down. He claimed he cared deeply for her. Melbalene and the man started writing back and forth.

Melbalene loved receiving these letters. They sounded like the stuff of fairy tales. He begged her to move back to Cleveland. He wrote that he would love to marry her. He wrote that he would buy a home and take care of her and her daughters forever, no matter what. Yes, this sounded like her very own fairy tale.

Melbalene eventually packed up her belongings and her daughters and moved back to Cleveland. The many letters made the man sound "like a prince" said their mother. The girls finally met the prince. He was a rather ordinary looking man. He was short with his hair shaved very close, which was called a "buzz." He had very big eyes that kind of bugged out and very thick glasses. His name was Jim.

Jim was older than Melbalene and had never been married. He was absolutely smitten with this beautiful woman. He lived with his elderly parents. In anticipation of Melbalene and her young daughters returning to Cleveland, he had the attic in his parents' home made into a spare room for them. This would be very temporary, he promised.

He explained that the three of them could live in the attic while he looked for a house to buy. That way his parents could get to know Melbalene and the girls. Once he found a house that Melbalene approved of, they could get married. He was, above all else, a man of his word.

Jim had enjoyed a good job for years now. He was not an alcoholic. He called Melbalene and her daughters "his girls" and was as kind as he could be. He soon found a house that Melbalene loved. They were married. His plan was coming together.

There was also a great surprise for us, our mother was pregnant. There was also a great surprise for Jim, our mother was not stable. In fact, she was very unstable.

Within weeks of giving birth to her baby girl, Debbie, Melbalene was in the hospital with a full blown and extreme mental breakdown. What a shock for Jim. The woman he loved, and the mother of his much wanted and beloved child was a schizophrenic with a long history of mental breakdowns. Vaughn had told him "she was just plain crazy" but hearing it and living it are two different things.

While Melbalene was in the hospital for an extended stay, her three daughters, Sandy, Brenda and new little baby, Deb, were cared for by Jim's parents. They took very good care of all three girls. They got Brenda and Sandy started in school. Jim's parents came to very much love Deb, their oldest and favorite son's (there were two others) first born child. They tried to bond with Melbalene's other two daughters, but the two girls really weren't family.

When Melbalene returned home to the new house she loved and had picked out, she did not know her daughters, Jim or baby Deb. How very sad for everyone. Jim was shocked and heartbroken with this turn of events. He was also vigilant with his wife and determined to make everything better. It was his nature.

He watched Melbalene closely and made sure she took her medications. He was very insistent every day on this issue. Sadly, despite his vigilance, his beautiful bride was not what he had expected or been prepared for. His fairy tale life was often a nightmare. He was a man of his word, however, and would do as he had promised.

If not for his daughter, Deb, Jim would not have stayed in this relationship for as long as he did, but he did stay. His little girl needed her mother. He would watch carefully to keep Deb safe. There was no fighting. There was no screaming. There was no hiding in the closet. There was no love.

Though Jim tried to prevent trauma in the household, Melbalene was in and out of mental hospitals every six to eight months for the next ten years. As usual, with every breakdown there was strange behavior from his wife that affected the three girls deeply. Neighbors were shocked and some simply pulled away. Others that were friends tried to stand by the family.

Despite these challenges Jim kept his word. He took care of Melbalene, her daughters and little Deb. They lived in a new home in a nice neighborhood. They were staying put, not moving every few months. This was the most stable ten years for Brenda and her sister, Sandy. It was such a healthy environment for them despite their mother's continued mental concerns.

Brenda and Sandy went to just one junior high and then just one high school. They made actual friends. It was the longest they'd stayed in one place, ever, and they were safe. There was a sad ripple effect going on though (or perhaps a tidal wave). With every breakdown Melbalene went through, the entire family was affected. Her three girls most especially.

When Deb was old enough to be left alone, Jim divorced Melbalene. He would always love this beautiful woman, the mother of his only child, but his constant vigilance and Melbalene's continuous breakdowns had exhausted him. It was no way to live. He got full custody of Deb, which was easy for him. On his side, he had ten years of proof of mental issues and medical records of Melbalene's psych stays at mental hospitals.

In those ten years, Brenda and Sandy began to grow apart and their relationship became very badly fractured. Meanwhile, they both also grew up and moved on, taking their own damaged souls and hidden demons with them. Also, in those ten years, Melbalene and Jim had

TALES OF MARRIAGES AND HOSPITALS

befriended a man who was quite happy about this most recent divorce. The man's name was Barney, or Byron, and he had loved Melbalene, according to him, "his whole life."

It was never known just how Jim and Barney may have met. When Barney was eventually invited to dinner at the home of Melbalene and Jim, Barney recognized Melbalene immediately. She was a young woman he knew in his hometown of Webster Springs, West Virginia. Barney claimed to have always loved Melbalene, but she was married to George at that time and to Jim now. What a small world we live in.

Barney had been married previously. When he found out the love of his life was married, he did marry someone else. They had a baby girl that survived only a week or so after birth. Barney's wife pined the loss of her baby so deeply, she herself died shortly after the loss of their little girl.

After Jim divorced Melbalene, she moved in with a very happy Barney. He would tell anyone that cared to hear that he'd always loved Melbalene. Barney would also tell anyone that cared to hear that he just knew God had brought them together after all these years. He vowed to love her always and prove how grateful he was for this second chance.

Although Jim had full custody of Deb, Melbalene did get to see her daughter regularly. Jim would never have kept them apart. But Deb was angry and hateful toward her mother. Deb had been hurt so much by her mother's unstable nature, and she'd been hurt even worse in light of her parents' divorce. Sadly, the stress of her youngest daughter's anger and hateful attitude plus her recent divorce from Jim, pushed Melbalene into another full-blown breakdown.

This was Barney's first of numerous psychotic episodes he managed in his many years with Melbalene. Despite the challenges of being with "the love of his life," Barneys' love story stayed true. With every breakdown Melbalene had, Barney would again repeat to anyone that cared to hear, the story of his undying love.

Brenda was married with three children of her own when her mother moved in with Barney sometime in 1975. Brenda had been heartbroken about the divorce from Jim, as he had been a good father to herself and Sandy. Not only was she losing her "father," her children were losing their grandfather, their Papa. Another broken family.

Barney made a promise to Brenda, "I will stay by your mother's side from this point on. I will never leave her or divorce her, no matter how many times she falls apart." Barney kept his promise, despite years of her mental breakdowns, and loved Melbalene to his last breath.

Mommy in the Window – 2001

That's my Mommy in the window
She loves me . . . . . . so they say
She didn't mean to do those things
That made them take her away.
We can't go in there where she is
So, we wave from here instead
That's my Mommy in the window
And she's not right in her head.
But she'll be home again real soon
We know this to be true
When your Mommy's in the window
Doesn't she come home to you?
She's not the same when she comes home
She doesn't remember things
Like the terrible stuff she did to us
That put nightmares in our dreams.
We stay with different people
Sometimes family, sometimes friends
They try to take good care of us
Until Mommy's home again.
Now Mommy's coming home today
My tummy hurts to hear
They say we shouldn't be afraid
Because "Mommy loves you dear"

We always say our prayers at night
Before we go to bed
But we never say God's name out loud
Because of what Mommy says.
She never has much to say of "Him"
But when she started acting strange
She said God gave her the strength
To do all those awful things.
That was a long, long time ago
Now I'm a Mommy too
I truly love my children
Never scared them through and through.
But my Mommy is in the window again
Again, she's locked inside
And my stomach feels like the little girl
That used to run and hide.
And I pray for strength to care for her
He'll forgive me as I forgive others
I say that prayer with all my heart
And with each word I think of my Mother.
Give me strength to do what is right
Though others are angry with me
For my Mommy's in the window again
Because that's where she needs to be.

Tales of Alcohol and Crimes

George and his friends overdid the drinking during the football game. After George drove his drunken friends' home in his beat-up old truck, he couldn't wait to return to the house and enjoy the rest of the evening. His wife had been very nice to his friends and they sure bragged about her cooking.

Melbalene had been very gracious the entire evening, considering she did not know he was bringing friends home to listen to the football game. She certainly didn't know about the horrible "secrets" going on in the basement, for ever so long.

When George started to pull into the driveway of the house, he saw a police car following behind him. He pulled away from the house and turned around. He had no intention of going into that house with the police there. George and the police had a very unfriendly history.

George drove a few miles and pulled into an alley. He was exhausted from his day and drunk from his drinking. He would take a little nap and then return to the house. He fell into a deep drunken sleep. He woke up the next day late for work. He had not even made it home last night to check on his family.

George drove to the house. He went inside to find no one home. Of course, his girls would be at school, but where was Melbalene? She rarely went anywhere without him. He called his workplace to say he would be late.

Just as he hung up the phone, there was a knock at the door. George opened the door to find an elderly neighbor standing there. The old man was the neighborhood snoop. Pretty much all he did was sit on his porch or peer out his front window and watch the activities of his neighbors.

The old man said, "They took your lovely wife and daughters."

George had no idea what the old man was saying. The old man continued, "First the police took them, then a woman drove them back here and your wife and daughters left with the woman. Your wife was carrying a suitcase."

George felt sick to his stomach. It was a sick feeling that had nothing to do with all the binge-drinking he had done last night. George felt faint and light-headed. The room started spinning around him. The old man said, "Are you okay there, young fella?"

George screamed at the old man to go away and he slammed the front door right in his face. George was shaking uncontrollably. He ran to the bathroom and stayed in there a long time just shaking and vomiting. George never got sick like this after drinking, this was something else. He had a deep dark feeling come over him. They were gone. He felt utterly alone and completely guilty.

Where was Melbalene? Where were his girls? Had he done something so terrible that his wife, his love, would leave? That can't be true, they had stuck together through so very many difficult times and Melbalene had always been there for him.

Melbalene had put the little family through so much with her unstable mental condition. George had been faithful to her always and had done his best to keep his family together, always.

George was finally able to leave the bathroom. He was still shaky and light-headed. What he needed was a drink. Before he could think any more about that drink he needed, he passed out on the floor.

Hours later there was a loud pounding at the front door. George stumbled to the door, still without that drink. He had every intention of screaming at the old snoopy neighbor but when he opened the door, two police officers were standing there.

The officers didn't even step into the house. They handcuffed George and one said, "You need to come in and talk with us down at the station." George was very much wishing that the snoopy old man had been at the door. He certainly did not feel like having any discussion with these officers.

TALES OF ALCOHOL AND CRIMES

The Cleveland Police knew George. They had arrested him on several occasions. The policemen that knew him best actually liked the personality he projected. He was educated and always very neat and clean. He was polite and friendly. He did seem like a man on a downward spiral though.

He had a history of petty thefts and break-ins. He had a history of being drunk and disorderly. He had been in jail a day or two here and there, but was quickly released. It seems he was well connected with people that could help him. Anyway, there were bigger crimes and criminals to deal with. But today, this was a very different problem.

At the police station George was led into a room. The two police officers waited there with him. Eventually, an older man came into the room and had George sit down. The man said he wanted to talk to George about his family. George was suddenly sick with fear and then just sick. Something terrible must have happened to his family.

Something terrible had happened. As the older man explained to George why the police had been called to the house the night before, George became ill, literally ill. They were saying that he had molested his precious little daughters. He would never do such a thing.

George screamed that they were wrong. He would never have done the sickening things of which they were accusing him. He explained that two of his co-workers were at his house last night listening to the game, it must have been one of them.

George was again shaking uncontrollably. He was again craving that drink desperately. The longer the older man spoke to George, the worse George was acting. It occurred to the three men in the room with him that he was in acute need of something for his nerves, he needed some medical attention.

George was taken to the hospital. He obviously needed to be checked out. He was shaking uncontrollably and kept passing out or blacking out. Whatever was happening to George, he was now in the hospital. He was at the same hospital where they had checked out his little girls.

George insisted on speaking to the doctors that examined his daughters. The doctors were not there, but one of the nurses who had assisted did come in to speak with George. The nurse was very cold toward George and would not say much. She certainly did not go into the same graphic detail with George that the older man at the police station had. She did finally say that Melbalene and her daughters were where they would be safe from him. Then in a stern and very forward tone the nurse said to George, "You need to stay away from them for the rest of your life."

George was at the hospital for more than a week. It was a difficult stay for several reasons. Any of the nurses or doctors that checked on him were very cold and aloof. He did not hear from the police anymore. He also did not hear from his wife or anything about his daughters.

When George was released from the hospital, he returned to the house. The place was too silent. It felt more than empty. It was vacant, abandoned, bleak and sad. George could not stay here. The dark was too deep. He went to a local and very familiar tavern and drank, a lot.

George laid his head down on the table and dozed off. He was emotionally drained. Someone was shaking him awake. It was a co-worker from his company. She asked George if he was alright. She asked where he'd been. She asked if he had called work yet. She said she was sorry but he'd lost his job and she began asking questions. There were more questions than George cared to answer, so he answered none of them.

George returned to the house. He packed up a couple things and then wandered around from room to room. He went into the kitchen and pictured Melbalene cooking. She was a wonderful cook. He loved her food. He loved her.

He went into their bedroom. They finally had a room away from their girls. He enjoyed being alone with Melbalene. She was to this day the most beautiful woman he had ever met, and she was his. Or was she? He still could not imagine that she had left him. It didn't make any sense to him at all. He was so completely lost.

He went to his daughters' room. They were his precious girls. They could not be gone. He could not live without them and their mother. He would not and could not stay in this house. He had to look for his family. He went to the basement to gather some tools he could not leave behind.

He stood in the basement at the bottom of the stairs. There was sunlight streaming through the basement window. The sunbeams shone on a stool in the far corner. A sick feeling came over George. This stool was where his little girls told the police the man had them stand and then molested them.

George pictured each young daughter standing on that stool in the basement. They must have been so terrified. Why didn't they yell out for help? Suddenly, George could picture himself standing right by that stool next to each daughter in turn.

George ran up the basement stairs. He left behind the tools that just a minute ago he could not leave behind. Those tools didn't matter. Nothing mattered. Without Melbalene and his girls he was lost. He left that house. He left everything in that house. He got into his old beat-up truck and simply started driving.

He wasn't sure where he was going. What he was sure of was that his family had probably gone to West Virginia. Melbalene and her girls were with her family, he was sure. He had to think of a way to get his little family back. He would tell Melbalene that he was sorry. He would tell his sweet young daughters he loved them and was so sorry.

He then recalled that the older man that had spoken with him at the police station, and the two policemen, said the little girls talked of being molested for years. That very strange sick feeling came over George again. This could not be true. It could not be him. Everything was lost to him if he had done these horrid acts.

If Melbalene was on the farm, she was perfectly safe. If he tried to visit her at the farm, he would be in danger. He would not be welcome, and her family would do whatever they could to protect Melbalene and her young girls. He was sure they had been told about the girls being molested. Melbalene's family would never let George near the girls. That family would literally shoot him dead if he came to the farm.

He had to think of something. He desperately needed a drink. A drink would help him think. He pulled over to a bar and had some Jack Daniels. He was soon passed out at a table in the far corner. So much for thinking. George began a complete and total downward spiral that day.

George's history of petty thefts and break-ins became his life. That history of drunk and disorderly was now a daily occurrence. George was no longer the neat and clean man from his past. He was dirty and unkempt. He was no longer polite and friendly, he was vulgar and angry. Nothing mattered but where and how to get that next drink. A couple of drinks would help him figure out what to do. Very soon, only the drinks mattered.

George lived out of his old beat-up truck. He did odd jobs when anyone would let him. He took money whenever he could. He was traveling all the time, not staying anywhere more than a day or two. When he was awake, he was drinking. When he was asleep, he dreamed of his beautiful wife and precious daughters. Both days and nights were nightmares.

One day he was compelled to get in touch with one of his brothers. He had not been home for years to see either his parents, who had rejected him repeatedly, or his siblings that probably wondered about him. After several failed attempts at phone calls, he connected with a brother.

The brother explained that he'd been trying to locate George for some time. He told George that their father was gravely ill, and that George should come home. "You don't have to worry about our father chasing you off, George; he hasn't the strength or the will, not any longer."

George did go home. He drove straight through to West Virginia without even stopping to drink. It was the first time in months that he'd gone a day without drinking. As he pulled into the long driveway leading to the farm, he passed the meadow where seven years ago his baby boy was buried.

George pulled over and began sobbing. He recalled that his baby boy died after he had struck his beautiful young wife in a drunken rage, knocking her down the stairs. Melbalene told everyone that she had tripped. Thoughts were racing through his mind. He began recalling other things that happened when he was drinking, like every bad experience in his life.

George composed himself and continued toward the family farmhouse. As he drove his old truck closer, he could see several siblings helping his elderly mother down the steps to greet him. George had eleven siblings and it looked like they were all there. There were also the spouses and lots of kids. He had been gone a long time.

His mother threw her frail skinny arms around her wayward son's neck. She was so tiny he had to stoop over for her to reach him. "Your Papa is gone," she said in broken English with her very strong German accent. Large tears fell down her thin haggard face. George and his father never got along, but his parents were devoted to each other since they were just young children in Germany.

George and his siblings were each born less than a year apart; his mother had a child every year for twelve years. As George looked around him, he realized that he looked twenty-five years older than his siblings instead of maybe ten years older than the youngest.

He was suddenly, and for the first time in a long time, concerned about his appearance. George was ashamed of how he looked. He hoped his dear mother could not smell the stale stink of liquor on his dirty clothes and body. He didn't even have clothes to change into. After bathing and shaving, he borrowed clothing from a brother. George was so skinny, the clothes just hung on him.

He was happy to be around his family. He'd always loved them very much. He couldn't bring himself to mourn the death of his father. If his father was living, he would not even be permitted in the old farmhouse with his family. He was on his best behavior, most especially for his mother.

George tried to hide the fact that he was shaking, almost uncontrollably. His body was missing the alcohol and he was in the throes of withdrawal. He never heard his siblings whispering about what was happening to him, but they did help him get through those first few days of shaking, sweating, headaches and vomiting.

Several days after he arrived at the farm, just as these symptoms started to ease up, his mother also passed away. She said two things often to her children and grandchildren in those brief days before her death. She first said, in her broken English, "I will not live without my love." The other thing she said was, "So happy my George is home." All the years his parents had been in the United States, neither ever learned to speak good English.

George's family of siblings had a service for their parents in the meadow near the farm. It was a large group of people with the siblings, spouses and children. There were now three graves there, George's parents and his baby boy.

George stayed on the farm for a week or so after his parents passed away. He had time to catch up with the family news. He explained that he and Melbalene were separated and he had come to reunite with her. He never said anything about what he'd been told had happened to his daughters or why Melbalene had left him.

A couple of his brothers had seen Melbalene in town. She was with one of her brothers and just said a quick hello and that she and George were separated, but that was all. George told his brothers that he would drive to Webster Springs the next day. Perhaps he would see Melbalene or one of her family. He did not explain to his family his fear of going to her family's farm.

George drove to town early the next morning.

He did not see Melbalene or his daughters, but one of her brothers saw George and followed him, blowing his horn and motioning him to pull over. This was the youngest of Melbalene's brothers so George was not too terribly intimidated—he was just a boy.

"You better stay away from my family, George, it isn't safe for you." The brother went on to say that Melbalene had gotten a divorce and the paperwork was at the farm as proof. He also went on to say that Melbalene had left the farm for a job somewhere and had taken the girls with her.

The brother had nothing else to say, or nothing that he cared to say. He told George that if he wanted more information, George could try visiting the farm and speak with the parents. They knew much more than he did. But he warned George, "The day you go to the farm may be your last day on God's earth."

George returned to his own family's farm. He was quiet and sullen. He did not share with anyone the warning he'd been given by Melbalene's young brother. He was too ashamed. He did tell his brothers he was leaving West Virginia. He was not sure of his plans, but he would be in touch. Well . . . that could be years.

George left the family farm the next day. He drove past the meadow where his parents and baby boy were buried. It was still a beautiful meadow, a nice resting place, but there was no rest for George. There was also no destination or plan. He was considering returning to Cleveland. He could find work in a bigger city or maybe just survive the best he could.

He stopped at a restaurant in town for a quick meal before he started his travels. Someone called his name as he sat at a table. One of his army buddies came right up and threw his arms around George. The big man holding George was teary-eyed. There is a special bond between men who have fought in wars and battles together.

They sat and enjoyed a meal, catching up on what they could. From their conversation, the army buddy realized that George had been having a rough time, a sour life and had a pretty good idea why. George looked twenty years older than his friend at the table.

Finally, his friend said, rather timidly, "George, you're the most intelligent man I ever had the pleasure of knowing. You served honorably in the army, you got a good education when you came home, you were the best singer and guitar player in your band. Your steel guitar playing alone could have made you a living. You were blessed with a beautiful wife and your precious girls. You had everything going for you, man. George, what the hell happened?"

Daddy Who

1981

I bet you didn't know, dear dad
That I write poetry.
Some poems are happy, some are sad
But each of them is me.
I've written of my love of life
And of my brush with grief.
And sometimes as a loving wife
To share my heart's belief.
Sometimes as "Mom" I hold my pen
To write about my kids.
To say some thoughts concerning them
And different things they did.
At other times, with pen in hand
I write a verse of love.
With praises for my wondrous man
A true gift from above,
Or I can write as if a child
Is my occupation.
And how I have been beguiled
By my heart's complications.

But of the many poems of mine
Of you there has not been
A single, solitary line
To wander from my pen.
Of course, I know you are my dad,
But my memory fails me,
For any love I may have had,
Has faded out completely.
You are a stranger to me now,
That's how you shall remain,
Cause no one ever told me how
To overcome the pain.
It's buried deep within my heart,
And I have no control,
Of feelings that these lines impart
And press upon my soul.
You say you want to know me, Dad,
I'm sorry that you do,
The only thought that I have had,
Is to stay away from you.

One Shall Rise

As a young girl, I had heard many times from both of my parents that "the family could be separated." It was often used as a threat to make us behave, to keep secrets, or to not question anything. That phrase was frightening. Being separated from my family seemed like the worst thing that could ever happen to me.

I discovered much later that my family unit when I was a little girl was the worst thing that could happen. Strangely, there was an unusual anxiety that came into play when the new reality finally set in. When sis and I were taken away from the abuse that we were so accustomed to, we were lost. My life became so strange without the screaming and yelling, without the constant fear and physical abuse. I was somehow missing my father.

Sandy also missed our father. We didn't speak of the abuse, but we did talk about our father on occasion. We talked about what he looked like. We wondered if he was looking for us and hoped he missed us also. Was he sorry for the bad things he had done? Why had he done such bad things to us? It was a vague reference to things we could not and would not speak of. To speak of them made them real.

We did not miss who he had become. We did not miss the foul smell of smoke and liquor that we had associated with him and his abuse. Sandy and I certainly did not miss the terrible secret fondling that our father insisted on. We did not miss the sight of our drunken unconscious father passed out on the floor with a smoldering cigarette stuck to his lip.

We missed the father who, during our first few years, would hold us on his lap and tell us we were his precious little girls. We missed the father that called for hugs from his little girls as soon as he arrived at home and walked through the door. We missed the father that used to love our mother.

After our mother divorced father, mother went a little crazy. Not her usual crazy though, perhaps a bit better this time. There were no hospital stays for ever so long. She seemed strong and happy. She made important decisions about her life with us. If things didn't work out, she would make different decisions to make things better for herself, and for Sandy and me.

Mother got her first paying job outside the house, which she was very proud of. She was determined to "start a new life with her daughters." She was going to "discover who she was, as she was not really sure." She was going to have "a good family someday for me and my daughters."

This road to self-discovery on the part of our mother was a rough road. During the three years after she divorced our father, there was still so much moving. Of course, sis and I were accustomed to being transient. We had always been constantly moving on.

After the divorce from father the three of us moved to West Virginia, then back to Cleveland. Then we moved to Illinois of all places, then back to Cleveland again. Every move involved a new man in mother's life. She was desperately trying to create a new family, and I guess a man in that life was a part of her plan.

Our mother seemed able to find boyfriends easily. She was a beautiful woman. They fell fast for her, which worked out perfectly for her own plans. She also married them shortly after she found them. The men liked mother a lot. That was not necessarily a good thing. She was desperately trying to create a good family life for the three of us. She thought it could happen instantly.

The most difficult part for Sandy and me during mother's self-discovery was getting accustomed to these new men in our mother's life. First, they were here, and shortly they were gone. Mother was married three times in just as many years. Sandy and I were expected to call each of these new men dad. The boyfriends went quickly from "uncle so-and-so" to dad. We did as we were told; every time we were told to do it, we would call the next man dad.

There was an Uncle Quinton who became "dad" for a minute. Then there was an Uncle Vaughn who became "dad" for a year or so. Between the uncles and the dads, the three of us would live with family or friends in different states, depending on where mother's "road to discovering herself" led.

At one point during this adventure, our mother was communicating by letter with a man named Jim. She read the letters to us. She would giggle and laugh like a girl getting a note from a boy at school. Jim wrote that he had loved our mother for a long time. He could not pursue her because she was then married to someone else.

He wrote that now that she was single, he wanted to be the one to marry her and be a father to Sandy and me. He wrote that he wanted to take care of the three of us. He would buy a beautiful new home. His fairy tale letters had won Sandy and me over right away. We were so young and silly. Eventually, he won our mother over too. She grew excited about his persistence and the prospect of being taken care of. She was soon compelled to return to Cleveland, again.

Mother told us to behave when we met Jim. We discovered the reason as soon as we met him. He was not as handsome as the other men in her life had been. He was not very tall (mother was considerably taller than he was). He was older than mother. He wore his hair in a buzz cut. He had eyes that bugged out of his head rather like an insect. He also wore very thick glasses that made his buggy eyes look even larger.

Of course, we behaved, but it was not easy. We could really have laughed at this strange-looking man. Mother told us, as usual, to call him "Uncle Jim." Jim surprised us and asked that we skip the uncle title and call him dad. After all, he said, "We will be getting married as soon as I buy us a house."

Jim was then, and from that day forward, a man of his word. He found a house that our mother loved. Sandy and I were so excited—a real home. As promised, Jim and our mother were married. He called the three of us "his girls" and would brag to everyone about his ready-made family. We were very happy, all four of us. A family at last.

A short time after Jim, mother and us girls moved into our new home, Jim brought a dog to that home for our family. Sandy and I were thrilled. She was not a puppy; she was an adult dachshund. She was not a miniature dachshund; she was a big, beautiful, black and tan female named Pepper.

Everyone enjoyed Pepper, she was part of the family. She was very smart and affectionate. She did not seem to have a favorite in the house. She spent time with each of us. Dogs are a lot of work. Sis and I would walk her. Our mother would feed her. Jim would bathe her and clean up the yard after her. We cared for her as a family and she was worth all the time and effort we put into her.

This was not the last pet to join the family. Over the years there was a rabbit, a parrot, several hamsters, and after Pepper was gone, another dog. Each of these pets that came into the family taught us so much. They were loved and cared for. They were important family members. They were such a wonderful part of our new life.

What a sharp contrast from the past experiences with animals was the experience in this new and normal life. I came to love and enjoy animals in ways I had never been permitted to explore. From that point on, my love for animals grew and creatures of many different types were welcomed into my heart.

The new normal in this life with our "dad" Jim, was a healthy, happy life. I very soon did not notice his strange appearance. I came to love and trust this man and this life. It was so stable. There was structure and balance. There was no constant moving. There were no drunken arguments. There was no screaming or hitting or hiding.

Very soon after Jim and mother married, there was a great and happy surprise for all of us. Our mother was going to have a baby. Very soon after the baby named Deb was born, there was a great and sad surprise for Jim. His beautiful new wife was not stable.

He did know of her history of mental instability but dealing with it was a more difficult challenge than he had anticipated. These were major nervous breakdowns. This would be the first of many break-downs Jim would dutifully deal with. He was a very dependable man.

I was twelve when little sis, Deb, was born. I loved the house that

Jim had bought. I loved the stable life he had created with my crazy mother. I loved the tree-lined neighborhood we lived in. I loved my new baby sister. I was so accustomed to mother's mental breakdowns, but I didn't even think about them. Jim took care of everything and did his best to protect us from the stress they may have caused us.

I did notice the toll it took on him as he took the full force of the stress. I no longer had to be afraid or hide. I didn't have to cry or worry. Jim took care of everything. I felt safe and was so happy. I no longer wondered about my father, George. Jim was a real father to me, Sandy and baby Deb.

It was a peaceful time, despite mother's constant mental concerns. Peaceful like nothing I had ever experienced. I made real friends, for the first time ever, in the beautiful neighborhood. I even made friends at school and was permitted to have them over. We were permitted to go to their homes also.

Sandy and I shared a nice big bedroom. Jim had bought us huge stuffed animals to set on our beds. Sandy and I each had bicycles that Jim bought for us. We loved to ride those bikes everywhere.

Jim had lots of rules and kept an eye on his girls and his baby daughter. We had so much freedom, but Jim was strict, and we had to follow lots of rules. I liked the structure and didn't mind the rules, Sandy not so much.

Jim never screamed or yelled or hit our mother. In fact, our mother even gave those things up after Jim came into our lives. Jim came home faithfully every evening after work. He was always sober and would enjoy the nice meals our mother prepared. He always complimented her cooking. The family sat around the table talking and laughing and disagreements did not turn into explosions.

Sandy and I had lots of friends now. Jim enjoyed having family parties and cook-outs almost every weekend when the weather was nice. The family most often included Jim's two brothers and their families, his parents and two widowed aunts. Jim invited our school and neighbor friends to join us. This was a completely different world than the harsh and abusive young childhood we had endured.

I liked school a lot and, for the first time ever, did well. I no longer hid behind long dark hair. I no longer cried every day I was away from home. I had good grades and enjoyed lots of friends. I was on the track team and the volleyball team, and I was very good at both.

I met my first love, Rich, at a dance at the YMCA that my high school friends enjoyed going to. He was a college student when I met him at the dance. I was so surprised how very much Rich seemed to like me and how nice he treated me. For some reason, I did not feel worthy of his sweet and patient attention.

Rich's life had always been extremely stable. His parents were married since they were young. He had two older brothers, married with families. His family had lived in the same house since he was a baby. Rich's family was Catholic and went to church every Sunday. I did try to explain to Rich that I was not good enough for such a stable, normal young man.

I was as honest with Rich as I could bring myself to be with what I dared to recall and share of my childhood. It was to no avail as Rich was smitten with me. How sweet was that? I loved Rich very much and was as attracted to his lifestyle, his family and his stability as I was to him. We dated for what I truly believed was "three fairy tale years."

I was not an easy girlfriend to have. I had extreme reactions to simple loving intimacy with Rich, which should have been normal between young loves. He was patient and understanding for a long time. Very soon I came to trust Rich completely.

When Rich got his college degree and I graduated from high school, we were married. We were married in his Catholic church. I had gone to classes, much to Rich's surprise and was baptized into the Catholic faith. My dear "father" Jim gave me away at the wedding, and why not? He'd been a good father for years.

I always felt that if Jim had not kept our family so stable for so many years, I would never have met Rich. I was always very grateful to Jim and told him so many times. I was more than happy to follow those strict rules Jim had set up all those years. I thrived in the regular, structured environment.

Shortly after the wedding we had a beautiful home built on three wooded acres. Rich was a good man. He worked hard every day and came home in the evenings, like clockwork. He enjoyed an occasional drink. He enjoyed cookouts and parties at our home and enjoyed entertaining with our many friends. I felt very blessed with this life.

My husband had a good solid job with a good company. I stayed home and took care of everything domestic. Although I really had no example to follow, I was very good at this wife and, eventually, mother thing. Over the next five years, our family grew, with the addition of three wonderful children—Michelle, Greg and Kathy. I enjoyed my children so much and was blessed to be a "stay at home mom." Rich and I had created a good life together.

I was saddened, though, that my husband wanted nothing to do with my mother. Even when she was stable and happy, Rich made it very difficult for me when I wanted to visit my mother. He was even more insistent that our children were not around her. I truly understood his concern, but my heart was broken over this demand from my husband.

During those very stable and happy years for me of school, dating, marriage, home and children, Jim was challenged and stressed, more than he ever shared with anyone. He had to always keep a watchful eye on his wife, my dear mother.

She was Jim's wife, the mother of his only child, his responsibility and his concern. Caring for her, no matter what, was important to him. Even when she had her horrible and very regular breakdowns, Jim handled everything. It was an exhausting and challenging life for him. He did not burden his girls with his challenges.

Occasionally I would recall my past abusive childhood. It seemed like a distant nightmare. It was like a horrible dream, all foggy and dim in the recesses of my mind. It was hard to believe that it was ever part of my life. The more time that went by, the more distant the nightmare became.

I never did really share those memories with any family, not even my husband, Rich. I most definitely did not discuss it with my many new friends. It was a tainted life that did not belong anywhere near my life as it was now. It was still, unfortunately, in the fabric of my soul.

I tried not to think of my father but would occasionally wonder where he was and what he was doing. I had family in West Virginia that would sometimes see one of my father's brothers (one of the uncles that I had never met) and would find out things about him. They would share the information when they visited family in Ohio. It was never good news about George.

As time went on, I became involved with our church, I was a eucharist minister. I was involved at my children's school, organizing mothers for the luncheon time supervision. My life was busy and happy. My children had the same kind of stable life that their father Rich had, and like Jim had given to me all those wonderful years. They had a beautiful home in a wonderful neighborhood. They had love and family and friends. Thank God that their life mirrored their father, Rich.

My children did not fear Rich or me. We were good parents. Our children were loved and cherished. They were safe and happy. These things seem so simple and easy. These are things that every child should have, but things I never had as a young child. I truly believed I'd broken the cycle of abuse I had known as a child.

Just how many children have a secret and abusive life that they keep hidden from everyone outside their home? How many men put their lust for liquor above the safety of their wife and children? How many women are beaten and battered every time that drunk man, who should cherish them, comes near them?

Probably more than anyone even realizes. It is not something that healthy, stable people and families would think about or question. It is also not something that unstable families, adults or children, would share. There is so much fear in these out-of-control lives.

I was concerned for my little sister, Debbie. Of course, Deb's father, Jim, was a good man. He was a good provider and a loving father to Deb. They lived in a nice neighborhood with friends and family nearby. But there was a concern. Deb had the same unstable mother with whom Sandy and I had grown up. Whatever Deb had gone through involving our mother, she had been alone.

One day I had a very unsettling vision come to my mind. I was suddenly overcome with a feeling of foreboding that I could not get past. It started suddenly on a very ordinary day, for no reason that I could comprehend.

I was casually watching my youngest daughter, Kathy, as she played. I thought how very much my youngest looked like me as a child. Suddenly, I had such a deep dark feeling of déjà vu come over me. Memories of past abuse, not recalled for years, came crashing back and slowly in the next several weeks, started to consume my every thought.

For Debbie from Brenda

1965

Little sister, in my heart, I know the words are there,
To tell you that I love you, to show you that I care.
I want to say your happiness, means so much to me,
I hope to find the perfect verse, that will let you see.
That my love is with you, wherever you may go,
No matter what you do in life, I just want you to know.
That in my heart you're special, I hold you very dear,
Each time I try to tell you, my thoughts are never clear.
My other sis is jealous, she doesn't understand,
I cannot tell you how I feel, her anger would be grand.
I've even said a prayer, to help me find a way,
To let you know I love you, today and every day.
But still I am not able, to say what's on my mind,
So, my thoughts shall be kept silent, and go undefined.
Until the time is right for me, to tell you how I feel,
I'll keep warm these special thoughts, and ever after real.

One Shall Fall

After our mother married Jim, Sandy and I had a different and wonderful life. It was practically storybook. We lived in a nice home. We went to a good school. We had lots of friends. We were safe and happy and had lots of freedom.

Jim had always been strict and kept a very watchful eye on us. Of course, he watched our mother most especially, as shortly after his baby daughter Deb was born, he discovered that his dear wife Melbalene was not well. She was emotionally unstable, whatever the circumstances around her. Jim was vigilant.

As Sandy got older, in her early teens, there were so many things about this new life that upset her. Sandy did not like that Jim kept such a close eye on his girls. "There are too many rules," she'd complain. She did not like that she and I shared a bedroom while our little sister, Deb, had her own room. She did not like the family parties because, as she said, "They're all Jim's family."

Sandy was vocally belligerent about the fact that this baby sister was occupying all our mother's attention. Sandy called Deb "the princess" and was angry with me for liking the little intruder. I loved our new baby sister. Sandy called me a traitor. Sandy was so angry. We were once so very close but started to quickly drift apart. Maybe it was a teen thing. Perhaps our tainted past was affecting our teen years.

Sandy would say she missed our father so much. She talked about him often. She became angry at our mother. She was very sure if mother had not had such severe mental issues then father would not have turned to alcohol to survive being with her.

Where was this foolishness coming from? I had never thought of these things. I could not relate to my sister's crazy way of thinking. We were heading down different paths that took us further and further away from each other. My very best friend, my sister, was soon a total stranger.

Sandy's anger toward our mother and Jim grew worse with every passing day. She was even angry that he was in our lives. When Jim tried to discipline Sandy she would scream, "You're not my father, you can't tell me what to do."

Sandy screamed a lot. We had been through so much when we were younger. Our life was so good now; had Sandy forgotten how things used to be?

I was shocked at Sandy's way of thinking. I was so surprised how differently she viewed this life that I truly thought was so good. Every time I cooperated with Jim, Sandy accused me of being a traitor. Sandy seemed to go out of her way to make me sad. I was heartbroken. I was missing my best friend, my sister, more every day.

I did not understand why Sandy was so angry. She seemed far more lost than she was happy. Sandy appeared jealous of my genuine happiness and our mother's constant attention toward our baby sister.

We had always been so close, through the very worst that life had to offer two little girls. It was a sad and sorry separation. It made no sense to me. We no longer shared each other's thoughts and feelings. We were no longer there for each other to get through regular teenage concerns. We chose different paths in this new life. Where I embraced it, Sandy stomped on it. At some point during this transitional trauma, I discovered my sister was drinking.

Sandy started stealing things from me. She stole money I'd earned at a summer job. Sandy would steal clothes that I'd bought with my own money. I would not have minded if she had just borrowed them, but she had to cut them down to fit herself. Sandy was four inches shorter than I and more petite.

There was a time Jim and I started a small "Indian Head" coin collection together. Sandy stole the nickels. She popped them right out of their nice case to buy cigarettes. Sandy would smoke in our room and empty her cigarette ashes between my bed sheets.

There was another real problem besides these terrible things that were going on between my sister and me. The worst problem was that I could never bring myself to tell our mother or Jim about any of these very upsetting occurrences. Maybe it was from all the years of protecting my sister, I could not bring myself to "tell."

Sandy knew very well that she could get away with anything where I was concerned. She had quite the hold over me. I was so foolish not to share my concerns with someone, anyone. Because of this, the problems kept escalating. Sandy was soon sneaking boys into our bedroom when she was sure I was asleep. Of course, I was not sleeping.

On other nights, Sandy would sneak out the bedroom window late at night and not return until morning. I was helpless to stop my sister. I would not tell Jim as I did not want him angry with her. I could not tell my mother as she had such a difficult time with stress.

Sandy's actions became more and more hurtful—even dangerous. One evening sis and I were alone in the house. We were arguing about something I do not recall. It escalated to screaming and fighting. Sandy took a lead pencil and jammed it into my leg and the lead is there to this very day.

Another evening during an argument, Sandy knocked me to the floor and put a knife to my throat. I was shocked at the look on my sister's face, I did not recognize her. I was truly afraid that Sandy would cause me harm. I did not say a word as the tears streamed down my face.

She finally dropped the knife screaming, "The only reason I won't cut you is I don't want mom to be pissed off." We argued often as teenagers, but I would have never hurt my sister; that was obviously not true where Sandy was concerned.

I was heartbroken over this very sad turn of events. Where was my sweet sister? Where was my best friend? Was Sandy lost in an emotional and confusing teenage transition? Worse yet, was it the alcohol that was taking my best and dearest companion away just as alcohol had transformed our father?

When Sandy discovered that I was dating someone, she would steal my boyfriends away from me—not because she was interested in them, but just because she could. Sandy was a particularly beautiful girl with big blue eyes, wavy long blonde hair and a full figure. Stealing the boys was so easy, especially since teenage boys are so dumb.

Sandy would say, right to their face, that she wasn't interested in them. She would literally laugh at them after they broke up with me. She just wanted to hurt me, her sister, her closest friend and best ally. In her eyes I was a traitor, but why? Was it because I had adjusted so well in this healthy environment?

Very soon, the stressful situation extended far beyond the bedroom we shared. Soon enough our mother discovered Sandy sneaking out. I got in so much more trouble for not telling my mom and Jim about this than Sandy did for doing these things. Shortly after mom and Jim discovered she was sneaking out she would not even bother to come home. When Sandy did come home, she would be drunk or hung over.

The stress level in our home was palpable. I would not even speak to Sandy any longer, which was a very uncomfortable climate in a shared bedroom. Jim tried his best to control my wild and wayward sister, to no avail. She was always screaming, "You are not my father!"

Mother was falling apart regularly. Jim was beside himself dealing with his home life. To make matters worse, it was soon apparent that little Deb was being neglected. That should have been no surprise considering Mom's constant depressed state.

Things went from bad to worse. Sandy was missing school often and soon declared to everyone that she would no longer go to school at all. Sandy was involved with a group of motorcycle riders that were very wild and carefree. Sandy was attracted to these bad boys. They were so exciting to her. She was fearless in pursuit of their lifestyle.

Sadly, if not inevitably, Sandy went from drinking to drinking and drugs. She went from hung over to stoned. Our mother and Jim were heartsick and helpless to save the young fifteen-year-old. Mother couldn't even save herself from her own demons.

Sandy ran away time and again. The only thing worse than having Sandy gone, was having her home. Her emotional discord and anger toward everyone affected the entire family. There was a time that she was gone a couple months. Mother begged Jim to please find Sandy, but he was reluctant to even bother.

When they eventually found my sister, she was pregnant. The biker who had gotten her pregnant wanted nothing to do with her. Sandy was living with another young biker, Ray, who claimed he cared and would take care of her and her unborn baby. Ray did seem to care.

At age sixteen, Sandy had her first child, a baby girl—the most beautiful baby. Sandy was but a child herself. Perhaps that's why Sandy and her firstborn were never close. From a very young age to this very day, Sandy and her firstborn daughter have never gotten along. She and Ray got married. A couple years later they had another baby girl.

Sandy and Ray lived a wild and wayward lifestyle. There was so much they enjoyed together but it always involved excessive drinking and various drugs. Within a couple years of marriage, Ray was beating Sandy. And so, the cycle of abuse went on.

One day our mother called Sandy several times and could not get in touch with her. Mother "had a bad feeling" and was extremely concerned. She understood perhaps more than anyone what it was like to live with an abusive husband.

Mother drove to Sandy and Ray's house. Sandy's two little girls were locked in a bedroom. Sandy had been beaten unconscious and locked in a closet. The return of the cycle of abuse was following the same play book and it was truly sickening. From that moment on, our mother helped Sandy come up with a plan to escape her abusive husband.

With the help of our mother, Sandy left Ray and took her young daughters out of state. As if it were the next chapter in the play book, she said it was the only way to assure that he would not follow her. She was in fear of her and her daughters' safety and even their lives. Mother had to do this same thing in her past. The cycle of abuse is hard to break. It is so sad that it can continue generation after generation.

Sandy moved to Colorado where a dear friend of hers had moved years before. Sandy was certain that Ray could not track her down in Colorado. The problem with this plan was that her dear friend was an alcoholic. Her alcoholic lady friend also owned a bar.

Sandy may have moved out of state, but she took her drug and drinking lifestyle with her. Her daughters were often neglected while Sandy was running wild in Colorado. She was able to divorce Ray while there. Sandy's lifestyle soon took a toll on her. She was not emotionally stable. Her little girls suffered in the care of their mother.

Sandy lived with several men over the next several years. She married a couple of these men quickly. Sandy was so much like our mother and she was unstable in her own right. The men that Sandy became involved with were abusive to her and her daughters. That cycle of abuse was becoming more and more familiar. Sandy was regularly beaten up by the men in her life. She seemed compelled to get involved with this type of man.

Our mother had never been a drinker, at least not to the point that you could say she was an alcoholic. Mother's unstable nature could possibly be traced back to the childhood trauma when she was terribly burned in a fire. Sandy developed the same mental disorders. She was diagnosed paranoid schizophrenic and bi-polar, both of which were secondary to alcohol and/or drug abuse.

It was so very sad that one of the traumas in Sandy's childhood would also become a trauma in her own daughters' childhood. Sandy was soon considered unstable and had to take medications to function. Her daughters suffered every trauma that having a crazy mother entailed.

These little girls were often neglected. They were often left alone— at times for extended hours, even days. They were often hungry. They suffered sexual abuse at the hands of the men in their mother's life. To make matters even worse, when her daughters told Sandy of the sexual abuse, she did nothing.

According to her daughters, their own mother said they were lying. Eventually, her oldest daughter, at a very young age, endured the heartbreak of abortion after being molested by one of Sandy's boyfriends. Soon after, her youngest daughter gave birth to a baby that she gave up for adoption.

Years later, Sandy herself told me these stories through tears and

ONE SHALL FALL

sobs. She was heartbroken that she had not protected her precious daughters, especially after enduring her own abusive childhood. She should have known better. She was beyond sad that she'd kept the abuse going for so many years. She should have learned from her own past.

Sandy's lifestyle led to decisions for her own abortions. She claimed to have had several. The pregnancies came at the wrong times by the wrong men. Sandy felt that terminating those tiny lives was the best decision for them, considering her broken lifestyle.

Sandy had crossed over into a far more abusive life than her own mother had ever endured. So much for free will. My sister told me many years later, when she was clean and sober, that she had prayed to God to forgive her for the loss of the innocent babies she'd chosen to abort.

Sandy was often out of touch with the world around her. Either she was drunk, high, or off medications that were needed to keep her stable. The cycle of abuse was ongoing in a second generation. She would sometimes choose not to take her meds, knowing full well what that could lead to—a lesson she had obviously not learned from our own mother.

But then again, did she even have a choice, given the awful examples, especially when she was very young . Sandy was a combination of the worst failings of both our parents. Sandy was a product of her past and her own misguided life decisions.

My own life was a good life but was also empty in so many ways. All the many years my sister and I were apart, as happy as I was, there was something missing: my dear sister, Sandy. We were separated not only by distance but by completely different lifestyles. Years went by during which we did not keep in touch at all.

After years of moving, drinking, drugs and men, somehow Sandy met someone who treated her well. His name was Jerry. She said he was like an old, laid back happy hippie. They were married (this was husband six and not the last, but who's counting?)

Jerry had a home in Colorado on a small plot of land and he owned horses. He was the first good father figure Sandy's girls had ever had. Together, Sandy, who was sober at this time in her life, and Jerry created a happy, long term relationship that was good for Sandy, her daughters and Jerry.

Sandy and her girls were introduced to the good side of the wild and beautiful world of Colorado. They learned about horses. Sandy once told me when she was first learning about horses, "Sis, I could ride a Harley motorcycle with the best of them, but I was scared to death to ride a horse."

Sandy and her girls were soon very adept at riding and caring for horses. It was a wonderful experience for them all. If even for a short time, Sandy and her girls bonded under the care and love of Jerry. Jerry was a patient man and a good man. Sandy and her daughters did so well for quite a long time.

In so many ways, my sister's abusive life mirrored our mother's. Sandy's own daughters went through so much abuse, even far worse than Sandy and I had endured. Why is it so difficult to break the cycles of abuse? Why can't we learn from what we ourselves have gone through?

Summer (says Sandy) 1963

So, this is it, a castle
With a princess, queen and king
But there is still this question
Answer this one thing.
What of the "other sisters"
In our servant space
Wearing "hand me downs"
Taking second place.
Don't upset the princess
Don't upset the king
Or we face the traitor
The angry "Mother" queen.
True this house is pretty
We never did have this
But I wish we were special
Me and my real Sis
I wish we had love
And someone to really care
But that is for the princess
And ask we do not dare.

Facing Past Demons

When my youngest daughter, Kathy, was about five years of age, I started to recall my very abusive childhood. I believe that these recollections started because my youngest looked so much like me. There was no other explanation. These memories were not something I cared to recall, yet I was helpless to banish them from my mind.

I had kept these dreadful memories at bay for decades. Now, I could not stop the flood of heartbreaking visions and nightmarish apparitions from sneaking into my every thought. My days and nights were invaded by them.

I was generally a very happy person, but these horrible memories were eroding my character. I found myself becoming the backward, shy and insecure child I used to be—but now, as a woman. I was drowning in a flood that was pushing me back in time. All of a sudden, the people that knew and loved me did not recognize me.

Over many years, I'd become a strong, secure, happy and healthy woman. I felt safe from the tarnishing influence of that long ago and distant abuse, and yet, after all these years, it was reaching out and affecting my life. Every part of my life.

My relationship with my husband, Rich, was undermined. I was distrustful and unforgiving toward him over things he'd recently been doing. I no longer believed in him as a man, or us as a couple. I questioned everything he said and did. These memories of my tortured childhood were ever so slowly unraveling my very happy marriage.

My relationship with my children became difficult. I was too protective. I didn't trust that they were safe with their friends or away from our home. I was watching them too closely and adversely affecting their faith in my love and my trust in them. People around me were

FACING PAST DEMONS

noticing that something was not quite right with me. Since they did not know my abusive past, they were at a loss to understand.

Unfortunately, I did not share the recurrence of these memories with my husband. Perhaps the years of not telling anyone about these abuses was too strong a part of me. Rich was at a loss to understand the change that had come over me. I did not seem happy with our home, with him, with our life or, at times, even with our precious children.

I had to do something, or I could lose everything. I had to face my demons. But how? I had to find my father. But how? I had to find the monster in my night terrors. Did I even have the strength? The very thought of facing him made me feel so weak and so frightened.

I had only seen him one time, years ago, after my mother had divorced him. I was about ten years of age. I was happily skipping and singing, heading home, alone on the sidewalk. It was on the street where my mother and her new husband, Jim, lived with his parents. A car drove up and stopped. The man leaned out of the car window and said, "Bunny, hello honey, it's your daddy."

I was terrified. I wet myself right there on that sidewalk. I started to cry, and it grew to a scream. I ran toward the house shaking uncontrollably, crying and yelling for my mother. Neighbors in the quiet neighborhood were stepping out onto their porches and peeking out windows. My mother and Jim came out of the house and ran toward me.

I pointed to the car speeding away down the street. "My father is in that car. He found us. He's going to get us, and bad things will happen," I screamed, over and over. My mother held me in her arms, staring toward the speeding car. My sister, Sandy, ran to the street and stood watching the car disappear. She started crying and shaking.

I became violently ill that evening. I sobbed and cried and threw up for hours. My sister took turns either holding my hand or looking out the window. It was a nightmare return to our life. My mother was frightened. Jim was very angry that his family was so upset and became very protective. He said, "I'll handle this." Jim was a man of his word.

As it turned out, Jim's father was a Cleveland policeman. Grandpa

Ralph ran a background check on my father. That is how we became aware of the fact that my father had a criminal record. Insult upon injury. This was the man I now had to find. An abusive father, a criminal, my personal monster.

I'd spent many a childhood night, after we were away from him, torn between missing him and hating what he had done. Hating him finally won out and I spent many private evenings literally praying to God that he would suffer for what he had done to my sister, my mother and me.

In my heart and in my mind, my birth father was evil incarnate. He was a large, scary, smelly vision seen through the eyes of a child carried in the heart of a woman. This vision of him was what my nightmares were made of. Now, at age thirty-five, I had to find him. I had to face my demon, my dad.

I finally got in touch with an uncle in West Virginia (my mother's brother). My uncle was able to speak with a brother of my father (oh wait, that was also an uncle) that lived in Webster Springs, West Virginia. Eventually, after several calls and inquiries, I got an address for my father. He lived in Columbus, Ohio, a few hour's drive away from me.

My husband, Rich, drove me to Columbus. By this point in time, I had shared a lot of my past and recent struggles with my husband. He had a better understanding of the sad change in his wife. He was anxious to see if this visit to my estranged father would help heal his wife and hopefully mend their shaky marriage.

We easily found the small gray house in a quiet neighborhood in Columbus. The neighborhood was very near a VA hospital. We discovered later that many of the people living in this area were veterans and lived here specifically to be near the Veterans Administration hospital.

When Rich parked in front of the house, I felt ill. I was dizzy and nauseous. We had not gotten in touch with my father ahead of time. I explained to Rich that I may not even have the courage to face him. I did not want him to know I was coming to Columbus, so I could simply leave if need be.

FACING PAST DEMONS

We circled the block a few times. My husband was so patient, considering this was nothing he could ever relate to. Rich had wonderful, loving parents and a good and happy childhood. There was no way he could ever understand. Finally, I composed myself enough to attempt to walk up those front steps. I asked my husband to wait in the car. I had to do this alone.

Rich insisted on accompanying me up those stairs and to the house. I was adamant, I told him if he insisted on coming with me, I simply would not go. Usually I would go along with whatever my husband wanted, but this was so different. Rich could not understand my determination to face these demons on my own. Eventually, he relented.

I felt so weak. I kept picturing myself as a little girl. It was like a strange "out of body" experience. There was a woman walking up those steps, but in my mind's-eye, it was a young frightened child that knocked on the door. I was not breathing. Fear of what was to come overwhelmed me. The door opened.

There before me was a small man, white haired, wrinkle-faced, hunched-over, frail. This was not my father. Where was my monster? Where was the demon I had to face? Where was the creature of my nightmares? Who was this pitiful person standing before me? In what sounded like a little girl's voice I inquired, "Does George live here?"

The little man looked closely at me. His eyes suddenly filled with tears. He covered his face and sobbed uncontrollably into a white handkerchief he held in his hand. Just as suddenly there was a woman by his side. She put her arm around him and said very sweetly, "It will be okay, George, this is your dream come true." What!?

I explained who I was and that I was looking for my father, George. The little white-haired lady said, "We know dear, we've been expecting you, please come in." It seems his brother (my uncle) had told them I was looking for him. She helped my father to a chair. I asked if my husband could come in also. I was not as brave as I thought I could be. "Of course, he can." The couple were very gracious to us both.

The four of us chatted for a while. As I stared at the shrunken man, he glanced at me occasionally but mostly did not look at me. When he did look up, I noticed he had beautiful blue eyes. Those eyes seemed to have so much sparkle and life in them; they didn't seem to match his sad old face. I still could not believe what I was seeing with my own eyes. He was so withered. He was so . . . . not scary.

The other thing I noticed was that he was now holding that handkerchief to his mouth. He saw me staring. I know it was rude, but I couldn't help myself. He quietly said, "I have an open area under my lip that drains all the time, I'm sorry." He excused himself and left the room for a short time.

When father walked away, the lady, Lily, said, "The VA hospital is trying to get him to come in. They told him weeks ago that he has cancer in his mouth. When his brother called to say that you were looking for him, he insisted on staying home in hopes that you'd come find him. I'm so grateful that you're here." Lily continued, "He prayed that you would come visit."

What!?

When my father returned to the room, Lily offered to make us lunch. "We'd love it if you'd please stay for lunch. I would be happy to make a nice lunch for all of us." Those beautiful blue eyes just lit up. My father was truly excited at the prospect of lunch together. I was feeling so strange, so conflicted. I immediately declined.

We did not visit for long. I was told the lady, Lily, was my father's wife of ten years. When I declined lunch, she insisted we have some milk and cookies before we left which we accepted. I could not eat the cookies nor drink the milk. I was having trouble with conversation, so I casually admired some plants in the room, there were a lot of them.

My father stood up and retrieved a pair of scissors. He began cutting pieces from the plants I had commented on. He put the pieces in a plastic bag and told me when I got home to put them in water. He went on to explain that they would root easily. He handed me the plastic bag.

His hands were shaking. The tears fell again down his face as he looked into my eyes. Those beautiful blue eyes. I could see and feel his pain. I was, by now, more conflicted. I was filled with sympathy, with hate, with sorrow and with love. With love?

A voice inside my head was screaming for me to say something or ask something of this man. I ignored the voice. I wanted to hug him. I wanted to scream at him and slap him. I felt sick. I had to leave, now.

We said our goodbyes. Lily said, "Please try to come back and good luck with your plants my dear."

The man, my father, held onto her arm, shaking. He could only nod in agreement. He could not bring himself to speak or to even look up at us.

Rich and I were silent in the car. After some time, I started to cry. I was filled with such a flood of emotions, I felt I was going to drown in tears right there in the car. Rich pulled the car over and just held me in his arms. He said nothing. What could he say? Again, so patient with something he would never understand.

After the flood of tears, I could not stop talking. Rich learned more about my tormented childhood in the three-hour drive home than he had ever known in our twenty plus years of knowing each other. I talked non-stop and was light-headed for not breathing. The flood gates had opened, and the words, thoughts and feelings came gushing out.

He had no choice but to listen to the forlorn tales and shocking revelations. He was trapped in the car with me. Sometimes he held the steering wheel so tight with anger that his knuckles turned white. Perhaps it was a good thing that he didn't know more when we were visiting. He did not say a word, but several times he drove along with tears of his own.

We really didn't speak of the trip to Columbus much after we returned home. I did put those plants in water, and they rooted, just as my father had said. I potted the plants and they flourished. I pondered why those plants did so well. They were beautiful. Why didn't they curl up and die? I always felt they should just die. Weren't they tainted by his touch?

I slowly started to feel much better. Strange though, nothing was resolved when I visited my father. No questions were asked. No explanations were given. No emotions were shared. But for some reason, I was better. I felt good and I was happy. The plants from my father's house continued to flourish.

There were no more nightmares. No more waking up, screaming of dreams locked in a closet. The flood of sad memories stopped eroding and invading my life. I had faced my demon, that frail sick old man. I did not need to ever visit my father again, ever. I vowed I never would see him, not ever. Then something happened and I had to plan another visit.

Struggle on the Streets

My sister, far away in Colorado, was having nightmares. She was waking in the night, screaming and terrified. I hadn't spoken to her in years as we drifted far apart with very different lifestyles. When she got in touch with me, I was so excited to hear from her. I loved my sister and being separated, whatever the reason, left an emptiness in my heart and in my life.

It was the strangest thing. My sister had been having terrible nightmares. She was dreaming about being a little girl and screaming and crying in the dark. Now the strangest thing was that we had not been in touch. She had no idea about my own emotional upsets while reliving and recalling that terrible childhood.

Interestingly, there was a common thread, my sister also had a young daughter of her own that looked like her. Sandy explained that as she noticed the strong resemblance of her daughter to her, the night terrors started. The nightmares had not yet stopped.

I explained to Sandy that I had found our father. I told her I had visited him, and the nightmares and night terrors had simply stopped. I asked her to please come to Ohio (she lived in Colorado) and she and I would confront him together. There was silence on the other end of the phone. Her voice suddenly became child-like as she said, "I can't face him." The phone went dead.

I did not have a number to call her back. We finally had spoken after all those years apart, and I ruined it. I could not stop thinking of her. I had so many unanswered questions about her family and her life. I loved my sister, I always had, and I had missed her so much. A few weeks after her phone call to me, she called again.

I picked up the ringing phone and a small, child-like voice said, "Okay, I'll go see him, but you have to come with me."

We both started to cry but did not discuss why we were crying. Sometimes there are just no words. We both knew the terrible past. We had lived it together. She told me she and her husband would make the arrangements to travel to Ohio. I told her I would contact our father.

Within a week or so, Sandy and her husband, Jerry, and her two daughters made the trip from Colorado to Ohio. After visiting Ohio family for a couple days, Sandy and I announced that we were going to Columbus to visit our father. Just Sandy and I would make the trip.

Our husbands were insistent that they come with us. Absolutely not, this was something we had to do on our own. This was something we had to do together. I explained to my husband that with my sister by my side, I would have the strength to face my father again, for her sake.

Our children stayed with their fathers and Sandy and I set out for Columbus. I drove and we talked, cried and laughed for the entire two-hour drive. We caught up on all those years we had been apart. We discussed our children, our husbands and our lives in the years we had been estranged. We did not speak of our childhood abuse or our father at all.

The time passed quickly and before we knew it, we were driving down the quiet street and approaching the small gray house. Sandy started to panic. "I can't breathe. I'm going to be sick. Don't stop, don't stop! Keep going please, Brenda," she sobbed.

I felt her pain and fear with every anguished sob.

"Pull over quick, I'm going to throw up," she yelled frantically. I pulled to the side of the street where Sandy vomited for a long time.

Sandy was pale and shaking. Tears were streaming down her face. She was crying so hard she could not catch her breath. We stayed pulled to the side of the road for quite a long time. Eventually she was calmer. "I'm sorry, sissy. I just can't do this, I just can't," she said. "I'm not like you, Brenda, I'll be worse if I see him, not better."

"Sandy, please be strong, I will be right there with you," I said encouragingly. "He's not the monster of our night terrors and you need to see that." Finally, she said she would try. We drove back and forth past the little gray house on the very quiet street for a couple of hours.

We pulled over several times and Sandy would get out of the car and throw up.

I don't think she actually gathered any courage. I truly believe she was just too exhausted to fight against my pleas any longer. I was very insistent about this, which was so out of character for me. I pushed her so hard. I just knew how much better I was after confronting father. I wanted my sister to be better too. I wanted my dear sister to heal. To leave without seeing him would haunt her as much, if not more, than her tainted childhood memories.

Finally, she relented. I helped her out of the car. I steadied her as we walked up the stairs of the house together, hand in hand. She was so weak I was practically carrying her. "I'm going to pass out," she whispered. I had an "out of body" vision again. I saw in my mind's eye two little girls, hand in hand, climbing those stairs.

We didn't even have a chance to knock on the door. The door opened in front of us and there stood the wrinkled, stooped, white haired man with endless tears streaming from the most beautiful blue eyes. I suddenly realized that my sister had those same blue eyes.

"My precious babies," he said in a very weak but very clear voice as he reached out toward Sandy. She crumbled sobbing into his arms. I did not expect that at all. I was sure she would have run screaming down those stairs and thrown up all over the yard. She simply crumpled in his arms, crying like the child she was in my vision.

When I went to put my arms around my sister, our father held us both. I felt like a little girl myself. At least that was the vision in my mind as I stood in the doorway in that hug with my eyes closed. It was a vision of two little girls in the arms of their father . . . .this time he was genuinely kind, and we were not afraid.

We could feel his love and deep emotion, both of us could.

From behind us a very cheerful voice interrupted the strange spell. "Girls, please come in, you must be hungry. We saw you driving back and forth, and we waited supper for you" (that was hours). Without hesitation Sandy and I sat at the dinner table with our father and his wife, Lily.

To this day I don't know what we ate at supper that evening but I do remember thinking it was delicious. Conversation was, at first, slow and painful. Soon we were all just chatting like the best of friends about all topics except the one painful topic that had haunted our entire lives. Sis and I were even laughing; this frail man at the table with us was rather funny. Didn't know that.

Our father excused himself several times during the meal. Throughout the meal he had held a handkerchief on his lower lip. At one point when he was away from the table, Lily leaned toward us and whispered, "Your father is extremely ill with a cancer; the doctors have been trying to get him into the VA hospital for weeks. He's refused to go because he said he was waiting for his girls. I'm so happy you are both here. God bless you. Your father prayed you would come visit."

It was late when we were done with supper. As we prepared to leave and return to Cleveland, Lily said, "Oh, please stay the night, we have a spare room."

The idea was completely out of the question. We had accomplished what we'd set out to do. We were free and clear to leave here and live "happily ever after."

To my surprise we both quickly and in unison agreed to stay the night. Where did that come from? When we called our husbands, they were shocked. They were both concerned and did not like the idea at all. They both wished they were with us. They both pleaded with us to return to Cleveland that very evening. We insisted on staying. We assured them we were fine because we were together. We said our goodbyes on the phone to our frantic husbands.

We chatted and talked for a short while after supper, but we were exhausted. Emotional stress will tire you out more than anything. Sandy and I excused ourselves and headed to the spare room. We could not sleep. It didn't matter that we were exhausted; our minds were racing and sleep eluded us. We lay there staring wide-eyed at each other, not saying a word. It was the strangest thing.

We heard someone in the front room, "I'm going to go see if that's father," said Sandy as she dressed. She left the bedroom. I could hear them talking and then I could hear laughter. I couldn't stay away any longer. I joined them at three in the morning in the front room of the little gray house on the quiet street.

"Dad was just taking out his steel guitar. I was going to come and get you, Brenda," my sister said, smiling ear to ear. When our father returned to the room, he was struggling with a very large and cumbersome leather case. "This is the only thing I ever saved from my youth," he said. "I was pretty good on the steel guitar back in the day."

Lily was now standing at their bedroom door smiling so kindly at her husband. I went to ask her to join us, but she held a finger to her lips and shook her head. It took a while for our father to set up his beautiful instrument. He explained that he hadn't played it for years, but he faithfully kept it polished and tuned correctly.

Suddenly, there was great magic in that room. He played that instrument so lovingly and beautifully. His entire demeanor changed. He was so happy and smiled at us as his fingers slid across the strings. He looked so young, no longer frail and weak. He was transformed before our eyes with his own beautiful music.

The most wonderful thing of all, he played "Amazing Grace," my grandmother's favorite gospel song. He then played one of my mothers' favorites, "If We Never Meet Again." Sandy and I were spellbound. He didn't just play his steel guitar, he was transformed by it. Sandy, me and Lily were crying while George, our father, was beyond joyful. Not only could he still play his beautiful instrument, he played it perfectly and flawlessly.

When he was done, Lily came into the room and held her husband, saying, "I had never heard him play in these ten years we've been together. If you girls hadn't come to visit, I may never have heard his beautiful music. I'm so happy that you girls are here. George has always missed his girls."

Lily went off to bed, commenting that it would soon be time to get up. Father very carefully, lovingly and slowly started to put his precious instrument away. He was so careful and cautious through the whole process. Sandy and I sat quietly waiting, glancing back and forth at each other. We didn't have to say anything; we both knew what the other was thinking.

Our father struggled to carry the awkward leather case to the dining room table where he gently set it down. He returned to the front room and sat down to look at us squarely in the eyes. I said, "Do you remember at all the terrible things you did to us and our mother?" Before he could answer Sandy said, "You beat up our mother, you molested Brenda and me, you ruined our lives."

Those big blue eyes looked right at us, their happy sparkle suddenly gone. His eyes now glistened bright with tears. Tears fell non-stop down his face. He didn't recoil at the question or the statement. He didn't look away or stammer when he spoke. "I've been haunted for a lifetime with those memories. I once thought they were nightmares, but when I became sober, I knew they were true."

"Your mother was the love of my life and I should have cherished her. You two girls were precious and blessed gifts that I should have protected and loved. There was a dark time in my life and a dark force that took over and I cannot go back and change anything."

He went on, "I don't know what to say to you girls. I can't find the words or gather my thoughts about those horrible things I did. I was a terrible drunkard back then that had crossed an evil line and walked on the dark side. It took years and several attempts to finally be sober and to have the strength to recognize and live with the knowledge of the truth of what I had done."

Sandy and I stood up. Neither of us had any words to express whatever feeling we were having. We stood there, hand in hand, looking at our father. We excused ourselves and said, "Good night." Sandy kissed his forehead. We went to bed and we both slept so soundly. I could hear my sister crying softly as she fell asleep. I fell asleep with tears in my eyes but no thoughts in my head. In just a couple hours we awoke to the smell of a country breakfast with bacon, eggs, hash browns and biscuits.

We both were actually really enjoying breakfast. It was strangely comfortable. Sandy was especially happy. I noticed during that late evening conversation how she'd hung on our father's every word. She put her hand on his. She rested her head on his shoulder. She had bonded with him far more than I. She'd forgiven him completely and was healing before my eyes. My heart was filled with joy for her, for us both.

During our breakfast conversation the subject of his cancer came up. Our father shared with us that he'd decided he was not going to the VA hospital for cancer treatment. He had put a lot of thought into it and just last night had shared with his wife that he wanted to stay home with her. "I have my reasons," he said adamantly.

My sister stared at the sick little man with the beautiful blue eyes. "No, no, no," she wailed. "I just got you back, I can't lose you again Daddy, please. Please Daddy, please." To say Sandy was heartbroken did not do this scene justice. She was mortified at the thought of losing him. "Please Daddy, please go to the hospital so they can help you. I don't want to lose you ever again."

Our father was shocked. This was not something he'd anticipated. He had not expected one of his daughters to beg him to fight this cancer battle. He was helpless to refuse her pitiful pleas. He promised to go to the hospital to see what they could do. He said he would do it for Sandy.

When we left, there were hugs all around. Our father was visibly shaken and said quietly through tears, "God must still love me because here you are, the answer to my only prayer." The goodbye was so surreal, almost dream-like. It was actually very difficult to walk away from our father.

As Sandy and I were heading toward the door, our father stopped us. "Girls, wait just a minute."

We turned as he walked quite unsteadily toward his bedroom. He returned carrying a large, tattered leather-covered Bible. He held that family Bible reverently in his hands, leafing through the pages carefully. Then he stopped to look at something tucked between the pages.

Whatever he was looking at seemed to have a great deal of meaning to him. He carefully removed it from between the pages of the large old Bible and handed it to me. There in my hand were four old bills, currency, from four different countries, the USA, France, Germany and Czechoslovakia.

I heard Lily give out a small gasp from behind my father. "I want you girls to have these. I wrote on them when I was just a boy stationed overseas in the war. They mean a lot to me and it is important that you have them."

You could tell by his expression and Lily's reaction that these bills were precious to him. (I have those bills to this very day and selfishly wish I had his old tattered, leather covered family Bible and his magical steel guitar.)

Sandy and I held hands as we walked to the car, not just because we loved each other; we were holding each other up. We looked back several times and waved. The old couple stood arm-in-arm on the porch. Both were teary-eyed as they waved back

Sandy and I did not speak much at the beginning of the drive home. We were lost in our own thoughts. When we did speak it was to comment on his beautiful blue eyes. Sandy was so tickled that she had our father's eyes. We were both amazed at the wonderful magical music of his steel guitar. We talked about the tattered "diary" on the bills from WWII.

We also spoke of how relieved we both were that we had confronted him. We talked about how sad it was—how very scary to start on that journey of confrontation. Such a weight had been lifted from both of us through the simple act of forgiveness. We were surprised how easy it came for us, the forgiveness, after we got past the initial terror of the idea of confrontation with our own personal monster.

We both agreed that it was unfortunate that we hadn't faced him years ago. Perhaps we could have healed at a much younger age, if only we had tracked him down. We were just not ready until right now, when our young daughters' resemblance to us brought back the memories of that abuse.

A Bible verse came to both of us at the same time. It was somewhere in Ecclesiastes: "To everything there is a season, and a time to every purpose under the heaven." It was also in a very popular song of the '70s that we both liked. The thought was like our very own sign as we drove together back to Cleveland.

After all these years, we were not afraid. The abuse was and always would be part of our past, but the fear was gone. We had faced our demons, together, as we had lived them. We did not feel tainted. After all, it had not been our fault. We were finally free from at least these past demons.

Losing Dad

Our husbands were, of course, relieved when we returned from our trip to Columbus. Sandy and I explained what had transpired during our stay with our father and his wife. They both listened patiently to the words of our story, without ever understanding the feelings Sandy and I had experienced and had shared.

Sandy, her girls and her husband, Jerry, returned to Colorado. Sandy and Jerry had met in Colorado. Years ago, they had fought together to be sober and drug free. They had a small farm in Colorado. They both enjoyed Sandy's two daughters. The family still had horses which her husband Jerry had taught them all to enjoy. I was happy for my sister, even more so as she returned to Colorado on her journey to healing.

After returning from Columbus, and the ordeal of facing my father, my life continued. As mentioned, I wish I could have faced him years ago, but the timing had not been right. I was surprised how free and happy I felt. I no longer dragged around the heavy burden of that abusive childhood. I had let it go. Of course, it was part of who I was, but I was well and happy.

I did not keep in touch with my father or Lily. I felt no need to build a relationship. The visit to my father had served its purpose. There was a small part of me that now felt I was a better, stronger person for having survived the abuse. Sandy, on the other hand, did keep in touch a little. She called on occasion to check on George and talk with him and Lily.

Sandy would give me updates when she and I spoke. Sandy was disappointed that I did not keep in touch with our father. Sandy and I were most definitely going to keep in touch with each other. We vowed that we would never ever go years without communicating. Being in touch with my sister was even more of value to me, in many ways, than facing my father.

According to the regular updates from Sandy, our father had gone through radiation treatments and chemotherapy for months, until his old body had maxed out on those medical procedures. Lily explained to Sandy that the radiation treatments had affected him in such a terrible way—his body was covered with huge watery boils.

Lily then spoke with Sandy and said that our father had agreed to undergo an extreme surgery to remove this cancer. Lily promised that as soon as George had healed from the surgery and was able to return to their home in Columbus, she would let us know. "Your father is very anxious to see you girls again," Lily excitedly explained.

A couple of weeks later, a rather nasty daughter of Lily's called Sandy and told her that "George does not want you girls to ever come visit him again, just stay away." Sandy called me distraught. She did not understand this nasty call from Lily's daughter.

Sandy had tried to speak with this daughter at the time of the call, but the woman hung up on her. We had no number to call the daughter and Lily was not answering her phone or returning messages. Sandy was distraught. She had faithfully kept in touch with Lily about our father and was heartbroken with this turn of events.

Sandy insisted on seeing our father. She explained that she was coming to Ohio and asked if we could go together again to Columbus and visit him. Of course, we would go to Columbus again. There was no way I could deny my heartbroken sister.

Sandy came to Ohio and we drove together to Columbus. It was nice to be with her again and the two-hour drive went by quickly. When we got to the little gray house, no one was home. We went to the house next door; there was no one there either.

A neighbor who had seen us knocking on the doors of the two houses came across the street to speak with us. He explained that Lily had not been well and was staying with a daughter (probably that nasty woman who had called Sandy). He did not know the daughter's name or how to get in touch with her.

He was a very nice and concerned man. He said he had always liked Lily and our father. He also explained that, as far as he knew, our father was still at the VA hospital. The nice neighbor gave us directions and we easily found the hospital, within a couple blocks of our father's home.

We spoke to the nurse at the front desk asking if we could visit George. She seemed a little puzzled and asked who we were. We explained that we were his daughters from out of town. She took us to his room and asked if we had visited since his surgery. We were both a little ashamed as we answered no and explained it was due to the distance.

The nurse was very patient and caring as she explained that our father was not doing well. She said the surgery was a long and difficult one and he had a hard time fighting through and surviving it. She tried to prepare us for what we were about to see. She said the surgery was extremely disfiguring. She explained that his tongue and bottom jaw had been removed and it was quite disturbing to him.

She explained that he was still covered with boils from a reaction to the radiation. She went on to say that after all he went through, they had not gotten all the cancer. He did not have long to live. Everything she said sent shock waves through us but still did not prepare us for what we were about to see.

As she opened the door to his room, she said "It is not easy to see him this way, don't be ashamed if his looks very much upset you. Are you sure you want to go in? I thought he didn't want anyone to see him this way." We explained that it was very important that we visit him as we had been estranged for so long. We assured her we would be just fine.

We were not fine. Nothing could have ever prepared us to see the sad and horrific sight before us. On the bed was a different monster than the one from our childhood nightmares. The huge boils were all over his body and were especially large on his face. You could not see his eyes as the nasty watery boils were so large.

You could hardly make out his nose among the swollen boils. Just beneath his upper lip was a long line of black stitches that went from ear to ear. There was nothing left of his face beneath his upper lip. The sight was beyond horrific. There was also a very noticeable smell in the room. It was a foul combination of medications and unhealthy flesh.

He had tubes down his throat and tubes into his stomach. He had IVs in both arms attached to bags of liquids hanging above his head on poles. There were more tubes running from various parts of his body. These tubes led to bags filled with different gruesome liquids, some red and some brown.

The bags of body fluids were attached to the bottom of his bed. They dangled there, each bag's contents looking worse than the others. He was connected to a very loud machine that was helping him breathe and another even noisier machine showing his temperature, heart-beat, respiration, etc.

The room was filled with a terrible stench that got worse with every second that we were in the room. The smell was a combination of human waste, disinfectants, chemicals, medicines and burnt or rotting skin. The combination of these horrific smells created the undeniable smell of death. It was all we could do not to vomit.

Sandy let out a horrible gasp that could almost be heard over the machines in the room. I could not breathe or make any sound at all. Sis and I backed out of the room, hand in hand, each steadying the other. We were both pale and in shock. We were truly horrified. He did not look human.

I looked at my sister just as she turned completely white and passed out on the floor. The very nice nurse was right there. She had waited outside the door to his room, concerned for our reaction, and rightfully so. "I should never have let you walk in there alone. I'm so very sorry," she said apologetically.

When Sandy was again conscious she began sobbing, "Did you see what I did to him? This is all my fault. I made our dad into a monster. He did this because I begged him. Oh, look what I've done, look what I've done." There was no controlling her sobs or consoling her heartbroken train of thought.

The nurse took us to a quiet, isolated room. I was so grateful for the solitude. My dear sister was hysterical. I was in muted shock. The nurse apologized again, "I should never have left you girls. I'm so sorry, will you be okay?"

"We'll be fine," I finally answered. "Please give us a little time, then we will leave."

A few minutes later, maybe it was hours, we were getting ready to leave. I spoke with the nurse, "Please don't tell our father we were here. He probably did not want us to see him this way. Maybe tell him we both called to check on him, and when he's ready for a visit, he can let us know."

On our ride home we did not speak for some time, but it was not a quiet ride as we both cried. The vision of our father that was stuck in both our minds made us shudder and shake non-stop. After we were a little more composed, we talked about how we wished we had never gone to Columbus this last time. We wished Lily's daughter had explained that our father did not want us to visit, because he did not want us to see him the way the surgery had left him. Sandy argued that we would have probably still gone to the hospital because she'd have insisted.

Sandy was beyond distraught. She felt responsible for our pitiful father in the hospital bed. "It was me, after all," she said, that begged him to go to the hospital. It was me who cried, 'I don't want to lose you again'." I felt just as responsible and I told her so. I explained that I had spent a lifetime praying that he would suffer for the abuse he'd inflicted on our family. The blame could be on me just as easily, if blame there had to be.

He was never ready for a visit. Father died two weeks after our trip to the hospital. The thought of him suffering like that for two more weeks haunted my sis and me. That horrible vision of him in that hospital bed was stuck in our minds for a very long time. Lily, strangely, died a week after her husband. On our couple of visits, she seemed so devoted to our father. I was grateful he had not been alone those last ten years.

This time it was I that got a short, curt call from one of Lily's daughters who explained that they had both passed away and said,

"I only called because my mother made me promise. We're spreading their ashes together." She did not say where the ashes were to be scattered. She hung up abruptly. I had no number to call her back and would probably have not called her anyway.

The world had changed, again. Sandy and I had different nightmares now. The vision of our father in that hospital bed haunted both of us for a long time. Sandy and I were both distraught over that vision. We wondered why he had to suffer so horrifically. Had we brought this on or had he brought this on himself? We felt responsible for the pain he suffered at the end, even after we had forgiven him.

After our father died, Sandy returned to her tainted lifestyle of drinking and drugging. How fragile we are. Her husband, Jerry, tried to help her to again be clean and sober to no avail. If the person with the drinking or drug abuse problem doesn't want to stop, it doesn't matter how many people who love her beg her to stop. Sandy and Jerry's marriage fell completely apart.

As for me, I could not be with my husband sexually after my father died. What kind of Freudian hell was this? I had always enjoyed my husband physically. I had never said no to his advances nor he to mine. I tried to explain to my husband what was happening to me. I was sure with time I would be just fine. I beseeched him to try to understand and to please be patient.

There was a problem with this. Because of my husband Rich's own past marital indiscretions, he instantly and mistakenly assumed I was involved with someone else. I was most definitely not involved with anyone else. Rich was the love of my life. We had been together for twenty-five years. I was in a strange healing phase that he could not understand or accept. He had no patience for my withdrawal from our sexual pleasures. My marriage fell apart.

Sandy and I used to wonder how our lives would have been if we'd not had an alcoholic father. How would our lives have been different or better if our alcoholic father had not become abusive toward our family? What if he had been sober and cared for our mother and loved us as a father should?

We used to talk about which was worse for our family where our father was concerned, his excessive drinking, his sexual abuse or his separation from us. We decided that seeing him in that hospital bed was the most traumatic thing we had ever experienced. That was probably because it was a newer more recent horror.

Sandy and I both, in our own way, felt responsible for how he died. I had always prayed he would suffer for what he had done to us. Sandy had begged him to please go to the hospital and fight the cancer. We both had our reasons for feeling responsible. Neither Sandy nor I were responsible for our father's terrible demise. There is so much in people's lives that they have no control over.

His drinking problem and subsequent abusive behavior affected us for our entire lives. It had a lot to do with who we were and who we became. My sister Sandy's excessive drinking and drug abuse affected her daughters their entire lives. Was this Sandy's own personal problem and life choice or an extension of the example from our father? The cycle continued.

As for me. I seemed to be doing just fine for years. I had a different life than that of my sister, a better life. She often commented on how blessed and fortunate I was. The only difference was that my damage was not as noticeable or as obvious as my dear sister's. It was hidden below the surface. My own personal damage was camouflaged by a good husband, wonderful children, a beautiful home, our church and our children's school.

I was just as damaged, maybe even more so. I was able to hide the damage I suffered from our traumatic childhood. It was just a matter of time before the damaged child would emerge from the facade of "happily ever after." When my youngest child was the same age that my childhood abuse escalated, everything came to the forefront.

Finding Dad

September 1983

So, there you are, the monster
That chased me in my dreams
The haunting vision from my past
The big and scary fiend.
I never knew you had blue eyes
Or a laugh that filled a room
I never thought you'd cry real tears
When with hate I was consumed.
You sat and listened patiently
As I recited lists of pain
That I was very sure you'd caused
From back when your terror reigned.
But here you are, a frail old man
Weak, with cancer taking hold
I prayed you'd suffer, and you do
How could I have been so cold?

I asked you why you hurt your girls
Tears streamed down your face
"I was such a drunk back then"
"I was lost before God's grace."
You said you gave up drinking
That it took a long, long time
You were ashamed to find us
Because of your vicious crimes.
Right then and there it happened
I just let it all go
Years of painful memories
I don't want them anymore.
I learned some things about you
Before you passed away
So much I learned, I really liked
There was a lot we had to say.
I walked away with one regret
About the short time we had
I wish effort had been made earlier
To get to know my sober Dad.

Losing Mom

As mentioned, Jim was a good man. He was an honorable man of his word. He took being the dutiful husband completely to heart. He cared for his beautiful wife, Melbalene, and their young daughter, Deb, the best he could for as long as he could. But everyone has a point in which the exhaustion sets in. It seemed the older mother got, the more often her breakdowns occurred and the more severe the episodes.

When our mother was told of our father's death, she said, "I'm sorry he suffered so much, but he really did deserve it." Sandy and I may have forgiven him for the abuse he'd caused us, but as a mother, our's could never and would never forgive him. I always thought that she felt a little responsible herself, as she always said she never knew what was going on between her husband and her little girls.

After my father's death, I tried to distance myself emotionally from my crazy mother. Dealing with one defunct parent had traumatized me more than I cared to admit. Every breakdown affected each of us that loved her, and I loved her. My heart went out to Jim and my little sister, Deb. I knew what a toll caring for mother took. I also knew what an adverse effect living with mother had on a child. I worried about Deb; she had no sibling there with her to cling to or talk to as Sandy and I had.

Despite my distancing myself, I also started to notice that my own children were being affected by their Nan Nan's constant hospital stays. I guess a child didn't have to live with her to be affected; they just had to know and love her.

It was difficult to explain to my young children when they would ask, "What's wrong with Nan-Nan?" It became even more distressing when we could not visit her for extended periods of time. She was either hospitalized or on the verge of a breakdown. She was often violent, something I did not want my children to see.

It occurred to me that just because my life was stable (or so I thought), I was not immune to the affect my mother's mental concerns had on me from the past all the way to the present. I often recalled old hurtful memories from my childhood that involved my mother. It was her own brand of abuse. I was angry that mother was now affecting my own children.

My husband, Rich, would often help my stepfather deal with the police, the paperwork and the hospitals. Rich also insisted that our children not be involved in any way, even to visit her. This crazy cycle of life could not be denied or hidden. Rich would sometimes accompany me when I visited mother in the hospital. There was one visit that comes to mind that was especially difficult.

When we arrived at the hospital, her nurse explained that mother was having a very bad day. "If you are at all uncomfortable during your visit, don't feel bad about just leaving," said the nurse. When Rich and I got to her room, she was sitting naked on her bed with her underwear on her head. Funny!? Not at the time! I was so embarrassed for myself and for her. She was always a lady, dignified and proper unless she was intentionally being silly or playful. Rich left her room out of respect. I followed him crying out of embarrassment for her and myself.

On occasion, when I was able to speak with her psychiatrists (and there had been many over the years) they could never tell me much as they were protecting her privacy. What a lot of bullshit! What they all said, and agreed upon, was that there was no "fixing her." Her best chance of living a more normal life was to stay on her medications.

I used to ask about those medications. Were the medications themselves causing her subsequent breakdowns to become worse over the years? Was it truly the natural progression of her mental illness? I was given answers to those questions in very vague replies such as, "It's hard to say", or "Medications affect different people in different ways," etc., etc., blah, blah, blah.

My mother never was one to drink alcohol, besides maybe an

occasional drink. I believe that drinking was not a good idea and/or just did not mix well, considering the strong psych medications she had to take. She never did recreational drugs, why would she?

For some reason, she hated the fact that she had to take her regular medications every day.

My mother did love her cigarettes and her coffee. I can picture her so clearly, sitting at her kitchen table, a cigarette in one hand and a cup of coffee in the other. There were days she would sit there for hours just staring blankly and only stood up to get another smoke or make herself more coffee.

In those fifteen years mother was married to Jim, she and I became very close. Surprising but true. Jim kept a close watch on her (making sure she took her medications and being aware of mood changes) to the point that she was stable most often. I very much enjoyed visiting her. She and I sat and chatted for hours while the kids played or when they were in school.

As an adult, when I noticed mother acting strange, I would tell my stepdad.. Jim always seemed to appreciate my input, often agreeing with me, and quickly getting her help. But this constant vigilance was taking a toll on him. I had seen this tired and exhausted response many times by many people.

It was a curse (or maybe a blessing) that I was acutely aware when my mother was heading toward emotional disaster. I was just as acutely aware when the people that cared for her and watched out for her were simply done.

When Jim finally initiated the divorce, I was extremely saddened, but I understood. I was especially sad for the fact that not only was I losing my "father;" my children were losing the only grandfather they had ever known. This became very evident when my sister, Deb, probably even more distraught over the divorce, decided she wanted nothing to do with not only her mother, but her mother's "other" daughters.

This was such a loss. Jim seemed helpless to do anything other than follow his precious daughter Deb's demands. He felt so guilty about the divorce, but Deb was now his main concern. Over the years Deb took full advantage of her father's sensitive feelings about his decision to divorce her mother.

Jim now had to deal with an entirely different crazy, Deb's. Deb was heartbroken. I know she was hurt and missed our mother. Deb became very selfish, controlling, manipulative and seemed determined to hurt and punish everyone in her life. It was difficult to have a relationship with Deb, there was such a high price to pay to be close to her.

Perhaps this was her reaction to her own deep hurt and loss in her own childhood. These characteristics were not a temporary reaction, they evolved into her personality. Maybe it was her way of protecting herself from ever being hurt again. But it also isolated her from people that loved her because, again, there was a high price to pay to be close to Deb.

After her divorce from Jim, mother moved in with Barney. They had a lot in common as they'd grown up in the same small town in West Virginia. They seemed so very happy together. Barney doted on my mother and she loved the attention. My mother took such good care of Barney and he bragged to everyone as to how wonderful she was.

Barney knew of her long sad history of mental problems, but he was sure that because he loved her so much, she would be just fine. That was not the case. Very soon Barney had to be just as vigilant as Jim had been. Barney called Jim several times throughout the months and years asking Jim what could be done to help his new wife. It was a strange setup.

Jim was soon a regular visitor at Barney and mother's home. The three of them were friends and were quite comfortable in this relationship. Jim helped Barney deal with mother and was truly compassionate toward what he knew Barney was going through.

Jim also got to see his ex-wife, whom he would always love. Deb was also less angry toward everyone around her, which was good for Jim and mother. My mother, on her good days, was the sweetest most caring person you could ever know. She had always made friends easily.

LOSING MOM

That is why people who knew her were so shocked when they saw her transition to her crazy side.

Several years after mother and Barney were married the strangest thing happened. I stopped by to visit one day after work. When I went into the house my mother and Barney were sitting at the kitchen table, the favorite gathering place in the house, with another man. I recognized the man but could not recall from where.

"Do you remember Vaughn?" mother asked me, "Barney and I ran into him at the grocery store. He lives just a couple blocks away." I couldn't believe it. Mother was married to Vaughn years ago and here he was at the kitchen table with her and her newest husband, Barney.

Despite Vaughn's age, you could tell that he'd been a very attractive man in the past. What a strange sight to see. Barney and mother's ex-husband sitting at the table talking and laughing like the best of buddies. But it gets even better or stranger. I would stop to visit and, there the foursome were, enjoying coffee and cigarettes together in that little kitchen. There would be my mother, her husband, Barney, and TWO ex-husbands, Jim and Vaughn.

Laughing, Barney would often say, "Too bad old George didn't live close. I'm sure he would love to join us." Barney had grown up with my father, George, in the town of Webster Springs, West Virginia. I always found it interesting that Barney was so comfortable with his wife's ex-husbands in his home. Barney was comfortable with anything that would make my mother happy.

People often thought Barney was a little slow. He still had a country twang—perhaps that was the misleading factor. Barney was a loyal and devoted husband to my mother. He was openly affectionate with her and she thrived on the attention. He was completely secure in their relationship. He was not one bit jealous of any attention mother received.

These three men would watch mother as she got them coffee and cake she'd made. She would laugh and talk, sharing safe conversation with husbands past and present. You could tell that every man at the table adored my mother, and my mother was soaking up the attention. Interesting that neither of these ex-husbands had ever remarried.

Vaughn was crippled and as time went on his condition just grew worse. Either Jim or Barney would pick Vaughn up at his home so that he could enjoy their weekly coffee and cake at mother and Barney's. When Vaughn was dying, my mother, Barney and Jim went together to say their last goodbyes. Three men brought together—their life with my mother in common.

Barney took good care of my mother. He spoiled her, trusted her and went along with anything that made her happy. Despite this, my heart was broken regarding everything he had to deal with as far as her mental health. It was like the same old remake of the same sad story with different settings and a different leading man.

When Jim also passed away, Mother was sad, as was Barney. Jim went to bed one evening and passed away quietly in his sleep. He had been a good friend to each of them. It may have been a strange relationship with my mother and her ex-husbands, but I believe it gave all of them closure to the past they'd endured together.

As with Jim, my mother had more stable times than not with her Barney. I was able to stay close to her and in a good relationship. I was again able to visit her often. My own marriage to my husband, Rich, had failed at this point. I was now married to my second husband, Larry.

Larry and I had been seeing each other after Rich and I divorced. We created a precious and beautiful daughter together, Alicia. She was such a surprise in my forties, and such a joy and blessing to my family and older children. Larry and I decided to get married and be a family.

Larry was a good man. He was hardworking and a wonderful father to our Alicia. Larry was also very sweet and caring where my mother was concerned. Larry would help my mother and Barney with anything they needed done at their home.

I lived close to my mother, as I had moved to Cleveland with Larry. My youngest, Alicia, and I would often walk to visit her. Alicia was closer to my mother than my other three children had ever had the chance to be. (Rich had insisted I keep our children away from her.)

Alicia was extremely bonded to her Nan Nan, my mother, probably because when she was a little girl, she was with me on every visit to my mother. Also, for a short time, my mother cared for Alicia when we were between day care "moms." Alicia also saw how much Larry and I loved and cared for her Nan. Mother and I even took annual trips to West Virginia with Alicia. There were so many good memories made during those years.

The breakdowns were always part of mother's life. They were dealt with the best that they could be by the people that loved her. It was just part of the cycle of life surrounding everyone that loved my mother.

As if she hadn't suffered enough, after all those years of mental issues, Mother was diagnosed with colon cancer. Dealing with cancer is a difficult challenge for anyone but combined with mental issues, everything becomes far more complicated.

Losing Mom Again

My mother went through the usual cancer fight with surgery, chemotherapy and radiation. She was so weakened from these constant procedures that she lay in bed helpless for months. Barney, of course, took care of her the best he could, always vowing to stay by her side.

She eventually healed from the surgery and regained her strength. As she got stronger, unfortunately, she became more and more violent with her breakdowns. We were told that the cancer had compromised her body to the point that she could no longer absorb her psych medications properly. At this time in her life that she willingly took her medications, they could not improve her mental condition as much because of her frail physical condition.

There was one day I went to check on her. I felt bad because neighbors and family were staying away—everyone except her long-haul trucker brother who visited her regularly. He even faithfully continued to visit when she was eventually placed in a nursing home. People are at a loss to know what to say to someone suffering from cancer, let alone constant mental instabilities.

Truly, I did not blame them at all for not visiting, (well, maybe at first). There were days I wished I could have stayed away myself. One day, my Alicia and I stopped by for a visit. She was outside doing "yard work" in her bra and panties. She was extremely irrational and mentally lost. I had to call Barney at his workplace immediately.

Mother followed me into the house and caught me on the phone. I hung up and said that I had to do some errands. Mother was extremely upset and asked that I leave Alicia with her and come back after my errands were done. I said I would take Alicia with me and we would both return later.

LOSING MOM AGAIN

Mother picked up a bat that Barney kept by the back door and started swinging it at me screaming, "Don't you trust me with my own granddaughter?" That bat was smacking full force just above my head (only because I had ducked) into the door jamb with every swing. I screamed for Alicia to run to the car as I tried without success to calm and control my mother.

Mother eventually chased me down the street in her bra and panties swinging that bat and screaming at the top of her lungs. We were not harmed this time. This was the worst I'd ever seen her act out with one of her precious grandchildren watching the entire scary scene.

Alicia and I were both traumatized. I tried to console my sweet daughter, wishing the whole time she had never seen her Nan in that extremely precarious condition. One or both of us could have been hurt. Mother's mental condition got so bad that Barney had to sleep in his car at night for fear she would harm him.

One evening he called me from the hospital. I assumed he was there for mother but as it turned out, he was admitted with a knife wound across his stomach. He explained that he had fallen asleep in the house. Mother attacked him with a knife, slicing across his stomach. He begged me not to tell anyone and promised he would get help to care for her.

When all was said and done, the cancer returned or was perhaps never truly gone. As it progressed, those of us that loved her wanted to be the ones to take care of her. However, that decision was out of our hands because mother was dangerous to herself and others. Eventually the police got involved after neighbors reported how crazy and dangerous she was acting. As it turned out, Barney had to place her in a nursing facility. He had no choice.

The entire matter ended up in court. The legal process was so very sad. I tried to get custody of mother to help Barney as he was so overwhelmed. As it turned out, the state of Ohio took custody of my own mother. She was a ward of the state of Ohio. I did not know they could even do such a thing.

The court determined we as a family were unable to make the right decisions for her care, based on the fact we had waited too long to get help. She was placed in a facility that was licensed to restrain their patients, because, for her own safety and the safety of others, she had to be restrained.

I was shocked by this ruling. I was embarrassed that the court had made this decision. I felt I had let my family and my own mother down. I was heartbroken that I had let Barney down. We had not seen this coming. But we were blessed by God because the person the court assigned to be her custodian always called us. She kept us completely informed and made sure we were involved in any decisions where mother was concerned.

Barney was heartbroken and felt ashamed that he had been unable to care for his wife that he loved so much. His love was not enough to protect her or the people around her. The last straw was when the nurses asked that he no longer visit his wife as mother was so extremely upset when he would leave her at the nursing home after a visit. She cried and carried on terribly every time he left, begging to return home with him.

My sister was living in Colorado and could not visit our mother, though she did call regularly to speak with her. Sandy called me often to check on how Mother was doing. Mother's court-appointed custodian even gave Sandy permission to speak with nurses at the facility. The nurses would regularly share information with Sandy.

Youngest sister, Deb, chose not to visit mother in the facility. Her main excuse was that it was difficult to visit with her five kids in tow. Now mother had practically raised the three youngest. How she would have loved to see those babies. I'm sure Deb had her reasons, but I was so angry that she had abandoned mother.

Deb also didn't call to speak with mother, who asked for her all the time. I visited mother regularly and at each visit she would cry for my sister, Deb, with me sitting right there in front of her. That was one of many things I had to learn to let go. I did try, though I may not have succeeded in forgiving my youngest sister.

Deb had been fortunate in her life, but if you spoke with her you would not know it. She had two loving parents that were always there for her, even when they themselves had divorced. After Deb's own two failed marriages (to the same man) and two beautiful sons, she met and married Ken.

Together they had three more beautiful children. Deb and Ken had twin girls and a son soon after. Mom and Jim doted on Deb. Mom would drive to Deb and Ken's home and care for the three youngest when Deb and Ken were too drunk to even get out of bed. Deb and Ken had their own share of alcoholic abuse against each other and neglect where their young children were concerned.

During those very difficult years Deb and mother were very close. Deb was, after all, mother's youngest daughter, her baby. Mother helped Deb every step of the way, often helped her financially and was always babysitting those 'precious grandbabies.'

After mother was placed in a nursing facility, she cried almost every day to see Deb and the grandbabies. Deb was too busy caring for those babies to visit. It was so sad. Mother missed her youngest daughter and that little family so much.

Mother was a challenge for the nursing staff. When she first arrived, she had to be restrained as she was so violent toward everyone around her. She also had a colostomy bag attached to her stomach.

When my mother became angry, she would yank that foul, stool-filled bag right off her stomach and throw it at the nursing staff. It was truly horrible and another good reason to restrain her. Eventually, whether she was just too weak or perhaps her medications had been corrected, she was back to her sweet self.

The staff eventually came to truly love her. She was the favorite resident to many of the staff and they would pamper their "southern princess" as they came to call her. Even when she was given more freedom to move about the facility, she preferred to stay in her room. Mother insisted on looking nice, wearing makeup and earrings regularly. Such a princess.

The nursing staff was very aware that mother would create stories on occasion, although in her mind they were true. Most of the staff was very patient with her and would go along with the wild things she'd say, as long as the stories were causing no harm to her or others. One day she started telling the staff that her nephew was riding in from New York to visit and he was head of a notorious motorcycle group.

The staff would smile and say, "That's nice, Melbalene." Little did they know it was the truth. During a phone call one day (which she was permitted to make) she begged her brother and her nephew, the only son of her long-haul trucking brother, to please come visit her. Early one morning the staff and residents of the nursing home were surprised when a dozen or so motorcyclists showed up to visit their "southern princess," Melbalene.

Now this was the roughest group of "wild side' young men that anyone at that nursing home had ever seen. With their long hair, leather chaps, black fringed leather jackets, boots and bandanas they were a sight to see. They were also the nicest, friendliest and most polite group to ever invade the nursing home. They showed up with dozens of cookies and flowers for everyone. What a sweet-talking group of hoodlums they were.

This was without a doubt, the most exciting day for Melbalene in many, many years. Not only did they visit Melbalene, they were speaking to every one of the old folks there, whether they were in wheelchairs, using walkers or walking with canes. The wild young men were smiling and chatting with everyone. Residents and staff, and most especially Melbalene, spoke of this visit for years. So much for making up stories.

My mother had good days and often extremely bad days. The more compromised her poor body was with the cancer, the less chance that her psychotropic drugs would keep her calm. There was an evening I visited at the nursing facility and found my mother severely angry, screaming and lashing out at me. She said horrible things. She accused me of stealing her belongings and her money, accused me of making up stories and causing the family to hate her. My heart was, of course, broken.

I was sobbing in the hallway of the nursing home, feeling like the little girl that had been so broken in my youth, and crying like that little girl from the past. I felt helpless and lost and so very sad. A very caring nurse approached me as I blurted out between sobs, "I don't know who my real mother is, that crazy woman screaming profanities at me right now or the sweet woman she can be at other times."

The nurse had come to know me over the past several months, as I was there almost every day. She looked at me in such a puzzled and matter-of-fact way and casually said, "Brenda, you know she is both those women. Today she is the crazy one. Please, honey, just go home and try again tomorrow."

Such wisdom on the nurse's part and a reality check for me.

As time went on and the cancer took over, mother was just too weak to lash out or fight. My Alicia and I visited her often, faithfully every other day, if not more. The facility where she stayed was located close to where we lived. Alicia would try to entertain her Nan Nan and get her to laugh or at least smile.

Alicia would sing or dance for her Nan. She would show her books and tell her stories. On some of our visits we would bring our standard poodle pup, Cory, with us. Alicia would practice training Cory right there in the room. Mother loved Cory and would often ask to hold the puppy in her arms as she lay in bed. She would try to talk us into leaving our puppy with her when our visit was over.

Soon she was at a point where she just lay in her bed. She would not or could not respond to anyone.

On one of our visits my Alicia was sitting in the bed with mother. She kept saying over and over, "Nan, I love you. I love you, Nan." She was holding mother's hand and had her sweet little face pressed close to her grandmother's pale white face. My mother turned her face toward Alicia and said as clear as could be, "I love you, Alicia." Those were the last words I ever heard my mother speak.

I had a bad feeling one evening. I called my husband to ask that he and Alicia meet me at the nursing facility. When I got there, the nurses explained that they were just going to call me. Mother was not doing at all well. It was just a matter of time. They had already called Barney.

I sat by my mother's side and held her hand. She did not talk and had no strength to argue or fight with me. Through tears, I told her I loved her, and I thanked her for teaching me to be a good person and a good mother. (Sometimes you learn what not to do from the examples in your life.) I sang the gospel hymns I had learned from my grandma, the same hymns my mother would sing, usually when she was having a breakdown.

My mother died that night as I held her hand and sang "The Lord's Prayer" to her. With her last breath, she turned her face toward me, and she was smiling when she passed away. Her face was calm and literally glowing. I felt blessed that I had been there.

I thanked God that I was with her. In my heart and mind, it was a gift. I thanked God for her. Larry and Alicia walked into the room just after she died. Of course, we cried that she was gone. We each loved her so very much.

Barney arrived right after Larry and Alicia. He walked to her bed sobbing, scooped her up into his arms and held onto mother and cried. It affected us deeply to see his pain. Of course, our falling tears renewed their torrent.

I called my sister, Deb, and she came with her husband and their children. I called my grown children, and each little family came to the nursing facility. The entire family held hands and said the "Our Father" together. Mother would have been so pleased.

Mother had paid for funeral services in anticipation of her death. She picked out the clothes and jewelry she wanted to wear, the music to be played, the hymns to be sung and Bible readings for each of her grandchildren. It was all quite grand. Again, she would have been pleased.

She'd made arrangements for an especially nice headstone to be set up in the family cemetery in West Virginia for her and Barney. When all was said and done, I took her ashes to her resting place at Fairview Cemetery in West Virginia.

After mother's death Barney would often come to visit us. It was just a short ride from his house to ours. There were many times when

LOSING MOM AGAIN

I arrived home from work after picking Alicia up from school, and Barney would be sitting on our porch. He was so lonesome and lost after mother died. One evening we sat on the porch and just chatted and visited with him. The whole time he was playing with a small object he had in his hands.

Finally, Barney said, "Alicia, I have something special I want to give to you." He took hold of Alicia's hand and gently placed a ring in her outstretched palm. "This is your Nan's wedding band and I want you to have it. You visited your Nan all the time and those visits meant so much to her." We were all crying big tears, remembering my mother. Barney stood and walked to his car, overcome with emotion that he did not want us to see.

My sister Sandy and her latest husband, Billy, drove in from Arkansas (where she now lived) a couple months later. Sandy had been unable to come to Ohio when our mother died as she was trying to recover from her divorce from Jerry and her return to alcoholism.

The three of us drove together to West Virginia. Sandy wanted to visit Mom's grave site at Fairview cemetery. Fairview cemetery was a beautiful remote place high up in the mountains. The view from every angle was breathtaking no matter the season. We were there in the fall just when the colors of the leaves were beginning to change, which made the view all the more beautiful.

It was a rainy day when we got to the cemetery. My sister collapsed at the sight of mother's headstone and sat down in the wet grass. I sat next to my sister and held her in my arms as she cried. It reminded me of the many times I had held my sister as we cried together as little children.

We were all weeping together in the beautiful resting place. The gentle rain came down mixing with the tears and running down faces. Sandy's latest and dearest husband, Billy, stood behind us, quietly playing gospel hymns on his guitar.

The goodbye at the cemetery was emotional for the three of us. In the strangest way, it was also very peaceful and rather perfect. Sandy and Billy returned to Arkansas shortly after. I've recalled our goodbye to our mother so many other times since that day, with the gentle rain and soft guitar music. Mother would have been pleased.

I got a call at my workplace a few months after mother died. A concerned neighbor called me to say that Barney had been sitting in his truck most of the day. I left work and drove to his home to check on him, as I'd been doing practically every day since mother died.

He was in the front seat of his truck, just as the neighbor had said. He looked so peaceful, sleeping in the truck my mother had bought for him years ago. I got into the seat next to him and put my hand on his arm. It was cold and stiff. He had died. I held onto his cold hand for just a short while and cried. He'd kept his promise to always stay with my mother. He did the best that he could, all things considered. I am sure the last living thought he had was of her.

I called the police. It took quite a while for them to arrive. I stayed in the truck with Barney until they finally showed up. I couldn't bring myself to abandon him. When the police did finally arrive, they called the coroner. It was so sad. It appeared that Barney had not taken any of his medications for weeks (he had been hiding them in a drawer). The coroner was sure this had contributed to his death. That, and mourning the loss of his precious Melbalene.

I handled everything after Barney's death. There was no one else. It was very simple. I did as he had wanted, had him cremated and his ashes buried in West Virginia next to mother. I had the beautiful headstone mother had ordered for them engraved with his name.

I went through all the things that were his and mother's at their home. This is always a difficult chore whenever anyone is entrusted with it. I sold the vehicles and their home. The whole process took an emotional toll on me. After taking care of everything, I shared any money left over, with my sisters.

Larry, of course, was there through the entire sad process as was my youngest daughter, Alicia. My sisters never helped, as one was out of town and one did not care to help. Deb always said it was too difficult with her three youngest children. Everything was too difficult for Deb.

Perhaps it was just too painful of a process for Deb to go through.

LOSING MOM AGAIN

I know it was for me. I made myself stop being upset that I had to take care of everything without the help of either sister. I just simply finished the entire sad process, with my husband and young daughter by my side.

I was at peace with the loss of my mother. Of course, it is always painful to lose the mother you love. I had always been there for her. I had long ago forgiven any abuse I suffered at her hands. "Honor thy mother and thy father" came to my mind often. I never knew if it was a thought or a request.

I spent time with mother when she was doing well. I stayed by her side when she had her terrible episodes and could have physically hurt me. I was with her often as cancer took its relentless and cruel hold on her frail, tortured body. I loved my mother and I was at peace with losing her. Thank you, God, that I was able to be there for her.

Losing Mom

August 5, 2002

I said goodbye to Mommy
Alone with her that night
She left to go to Heaven
As I held her hands so tight.
I'd come to sit with her again
As I had times before
I could sit with her for hours now
She couldn't chase me off anymore.
That night I sang so many songs
She'd taught me as a girl
And as I sang the prayer "Our Father"
My Mommy left this world.
Mommy's eyes got big and bright
Her face had such a glow
And then her last breath left her
But I did not let go.

I thanked my heavenly Father
For taking Mommy home
And then I thanked him even more
That I was with her when she'd gone.
God knows how much we loved her
He knew what she'd been through
And although we may not know it
He was there with me and you.
She'd tested us and tried us
For she was sent from above
To show us all the meaning
Of God's true and patient Love.
So, thank you God for Melbalene
For she was like no other
And especially God I thank you
That you chose her as my Mother.

Tears and Rain
(Sandy says goodbye.)

May 2004

Where clouds of gray covered the day,
To match the color of her saddened soul.
And deep the passions felt by Sandra Kay,
To say goodbye to Mommy took a toll.
Flowers so tall and angels small,
She brought with her to help say her goodbye.
But oh, so overcome she was by all,
And crumpling to the ground began to cry.
Her tears they fell, and more they fell,
But not enough to show how deep the pain,
And sobs so loud, our God heard tell,
She needed help, so he sent the rain.
Sobs from her heart tore me apart,
And all the pain I'd felt was none to this.
Though she was far, from grief Mom's death impart,
I want to heal her hurt with Sister's kiss.
And then a hymn was played by him,
"A Closer Walk With Thee," by her new love.
And mingled with the mountain mist so dim,
Surrounded her with blessings from above.
My Father dear, please stay so near,
Hold tight my Sister's hand, from this time on.
Protect her from all pain and fear,
And never ever let her walk alone.

Flowers and Angels
(Sandy says goodbye.)

May 2004

We went to say goodbye to Mom, together hand in hand,
Sandy's been away so long, but we're Sisters once again.
We've spent some time the last few days, first time without our Mom,
Together we will see this place, where I brought Mommy home.
I love this hilltop resting place, so much family's resting here,
It's beautiful and quiet, and peaceful beyond real.
Sky is gray with clouds, grass is damp from rain,
We are at this resting-place, for closure from the pain.
The silence has been broken, with sobs from my Sister,
She leans against Mom's headstone, oh how she has missed her.
While heart-wrenching sobs came from her, Billy plays a hymn,
On his old guitar, that he has brought along with him.
"Just a Closer Walk, With Thee," fills the country air,
I hold my Sister close to me, for her pain to share.
Billy sings behind us, as we sit there holding tight,
Memories flood over us, with full force and might.
Lifetimes have been lived and different paths taken
Years have swept by quickly, sometimes our love forsaken.
But on this special day, holding each other near,
Our love has no bounds, we know each of us is dear.
Billy's singing ends, he holds his Sandy, filled with love,
The rain starts coming down, like teardrops from above.
We leave this "resting-place," emotionally drained,
Accompanied by thunder, and the cleansing rain.
God had been there with us, on that special day,
He felt our pain, and heard the sobs, and washed our tears away.
Someday we'll see our Mom again, that is a promise true,
God be with my Sister dear and be with me too.

Journeys

I have heard it said when it comes to our lives, "it's not the destination that truly matters, it is the journey." I like that, except for the fact that at this point in my life, my journey is closer to the end than the beginning. At this time in my life, as I write this book, I know I am blessed. I have overcome so much and am a happy, positive and productive person.

I am blessed with a loving family. I have talents and interests that I enjoy. I have God in my life, my chosen friend and lifelong companion. I thank God every day for my many blessings and pray for the strength to always appreciate and nurture them.

Our lives are not just one journey but are made up of several from the moment we are born until our last breath. With every epic event and every major decision that we make, we are at a fork in the road deciding which path to take. Our life is made up of the journeys we take and the paths and choices we make along the way. Whether they be good or bad, the paths and choices are ultimately ours.

My abusive childhood took place during a span of about ten years, my first ten years on this earth. I carried the effect of those few years with me for my entire life, even to this very day. Those years affected me in every area of my life and came into play with every decision I've ever made. I did not know how to heal; the wounds of the abuse were a part of me, in my heart and soul. I will say, writing this book has helped me heal. I didn't even realize I was still healing. Perhaps it is a forever process.

Despite the abuse, by the time each of my parents died, I loved them. I certainly loved who they could have been. I had long since forgiven them of the horrific childhood that no child should have to endure or suffer through. I used to wonder who I would have been if my father had not been an abusive alcoholic or my mother had not been dangerously unstable mentally. I never have imagined a life with different parents, just simply a good life with the parents I was given.

There are many decisions I made in my life that had nothing to do with what I was taught as a young person. Many of those decisions were based on lessons I learned about what not to do. I cherished my children from the moment I knew I carried each precious life inside me. I always told my children I loved them.

I have never beaten my children. I certainly never left them alone or locked them in closets. With every day that I cared for and loved my children, I was, of course, reminded of my abusive childhood. There was never any way to escape my sad beginning, but I could break the cycle.

Sadly, my beautiful firstborn daughter, Michelle, died at the age of twenty-two. The mysterious shooting that took her life haunts me to this day. My dear son, Greg, left this earth by his own hand when he was forty-one. He had so much to offer. I was so angry and lost at losing him. I had survived a terrible childhood, yet I have outlived two of my precious children that I loved and nurtured with all my heart. I don't try to understand that any longer. The question could haunt you relentlessly if you let it.

There were decisions in my life that I know for a fact I made because of my very lost and broken parents. I was afraid to lose control if I was drunk, so I chose not to drink in excess. I had such a fear that I would do unspeakable things to myself or to my children, if I ever headed down that dark and unforgiving path. These decisions had nothing to do with will power; they quite simply had everything to do with fear—the fear of repeating an abusive cycle in my own children's lives.

Unfortunately, I was not very compassionate toward people with any addiction problem, whether the addiction was alcohol or drugs. I was angry that my family had headed down this dark path. I had no sympathy or empathy. I figured, if I was strong enough to say no, so should they be. Then my own son, whom I loved so much, fell victim to his own alcohol problems. My concern could not heal him, and my love could not save him.

He tried to control his drinking several times. He was so pleased and did so well those several times he was strong enough to give up his excessive drinking. Those sober periods in his life never lasted very long despite his hard-fought battles. My own granddaughters, his beautiful daughters, told me themselves how wonderful their father was to be around when he was sober.

I lost my son due to his drinking problem. When his drinking got out of control that very last time, he took his own life. I always told him I loved him, but my love and the love of everyone around him could not save him. He left behind those three beautiful daughters. Their love for their father could not save him.

I lost my father, my sisters and my son to alcohol abuse and addiction. Their lives, that could have been good lives, were affected in the worst of ways. Every person that they loved was negatively affected by their alcohol addiction. This involved a full four generations of various abuse. Their wonderful potential was never fulfilled, just lost in a bottle of alcohol or a container of pills.

When I look back now to my hurtful and sad childhood, I truly know that those difficult times in my life helped me become who I am today. I thank God for my life, and for every experience that got me to where I am today. I like who I am today and although my journey is not yet over I have traveled a long way to get to where I am.

There have been many paths chosen and many new journeys started. I have kept God with me along each of my life's paths, even as a child. I always feel that I am at this point in my life for a reason or a calling that I have yet to discover. Do I search for the reason, or will my journey guide me to that calling over time?

It would be wonderful if even one person with a terrible addiction—a father or mother, a husband or wife, a brother or sister—will someday read this book and get help? If the words in this book enables just one person to make the decision to get the help they need, thank you, God.

I know I am blessed. I thank God every morning for my health, happiness and family. I pray that I always appreciate and nurture these blessings. Though I say this, please understand, my life has not been easy. There have been many losses and challenges, but with God's help (when I didn't shut Him out) I have made it to the other side of every one of those losses and challenges so far and am stronger for it. Life is so worthwhile. Life is so precious.

I do need to mention my sister, Sandy. I love my sister, always have and always will. We have a connection like no one else in our lives, because we went through that horrible childhood together. We know each other's stories and share each other's hearts, thoughts and memories, but we took different paths in our lives.

When we were in our teens, Sandy had a very difficult take on the world around her. She went through changes and choices that I did not understand, and I eventually lost my very best friend. Where we were once inseparable as little girls, in our teens we couldn't even share a room without fighting and arguing. I was so conflicted about my beloved dear sister when we were teenagers. I loved her and I hated her. I missed her and wanted her gone. She made what could have been a very good life very difficult.

Where I chose to be sober, my sister chose to drink and even added drug use to her life. From her early teens she started down the wrong path. Her very young teenage involvement with alcohol was already destroying parts of her life.

There were stretches of time over the years when she was clean and sober. She always admitted she was so much happier when she gave up those abusive habits. Sadly, she always returned to the pitiful life-altering choices. Her drinking and drugs took their toll—on her life and eventually on her mind.

When Sandy was in her early teens, we were told that she was extremely intelligent. "Oh great," I remember thinking at the time, "not only is she absolutely beautiful, she's really very smart." She had the very best of each of our parents. Our handsome father was extremely intelligent. Our sweet and loving mother was a true natural beauty. But her life choices soon caught up with her. Her intelligence and beauty were lost in alcohol and wasted with drug use.

My sister Sandy is currently in a nursing facility. She cannot be independent because she stops taking her medications. When she stops taking her medications, she starts drinking. She took on the worst traits of both our parents. She has the same diagnosis as our mother, paranoid schizophrenia, but Sandy's problems are secondary to alcohol and drug abuse. She has even added a couple of her very own unique mental diagnoses with bipolar disorder and manic depression.

I talk to my sister often. I love her and I love to hear her voice. As did our mother, my sister has very good days, but evenings are difficult for her. She suffers from extreme sun downers, an illness that brings her diagnoses to the forefront in the evenings. She is in a beautiful nursing facility in Arkansas. To date, neither of her daughters have anything to do with her. I'm sure they have their own memories of hell with their alcoholic mother. I pray that changes. I wish they would visit her. I wish they would forgive her.

As for my sister, Deb, we don't keep in touch much. Some people are so difficult to be around, it is better to distance yourself from them. It is, at this time, a choice that some of her adult children have also made. It is strange that you can love a person but still choose to stay away from the harm they can do.

Deb is still with her husband, Ken. This is Deb's third marriage as she married her first husband twice. It was a foolish decision made by a young insecure girl. It is a true blessing and miracle that Deb and Ken are together. Ken is a good man. Deb and Ken were alcoholics for years; it's nice they have each other. I'm sure their children have their own stories.

I always felt the part in the prayer "Our Father who art in Heaven . . ." that asks that we forgive as we want to be forgiven, was difficult. When I was finally able to forgive my parents, my life and myself were so much better. My many blessings came to the forefront of my life. Too bad I was unable to forgive my parents when I was younger. Perhaps my nieces, both my sister's daughters, are just not ready to forgive their mother right now.

I'm sad Sandy is so alone. When her last husband, Billy, (husband number seven) passed away, Sandy was completely alone. He loved her very much and took good care of her. My heart breaks when she begs me to come and get her. I cannot and will not. I took care of one crazy woman and I don't have the strength to care for another. I refuse to even try.

Sandy has some very good days. I've had conversations with my dear sister and have told her that I cannot take care of her and I have told her why.

"It's okay, sis," she says to me. "I understand. I will always love you, Brenda. Please remember that, promise me, Sis." Sandy begs. Her understanding makes my decision not to care for her hurt ever more painfully.

If we weren't separated by states (I am in Ohio while she's in Arkansas under the care of that state) I would visit her often. The last time I saw her, she was so weak and sick, she reminded me of our mother. My dear sister seems far older than I, even though she is younger by a year. It's not the years that have aged her; it is her life's choices, her chosen paths and journeys.

Sandy has always had great faith in God. She has said that she knew his love was always there. She knew his teachings, but she chose to do whatever she wanted. She has said that God is probably disappointed in her, but she knows he loves her and has forgiven her like any good parent would forgive their own child.

God is like a loving parent. His teachings and the examples of His son Jesus can guide us and direct us but eventually we will make our own decisions. We will choose our own path, with or without Him. That "free will' can get us into trouble.

Like any loving parent, when our child goes astray, we are heartbroken and sad. We have loved them and taught them well and they choose a wrong path. Of course, we still love them. We wait for the day they straighten themselves out, as only they can, if ever they do.

Sandy misses her daughters but does not blame them for staying away. Sandy accepts that she made mistakes in her life. I am so proud of my sister for never having blamed others for the paths she chose to take. But there are many times, as I myself have wondered, who could she have been if she'd been blessed with loving parents? Where would her intelligence and beauty have taken her?

Be strong and be brave. Say no to evil ways. Keep God, your forever friend, close to you. Love your children. Love them truly and love them gently in ways you can proudly and openly share with the world. Love your parents and forgive their many shortcomings, be they real or imagined.

Grow to be the wonderful and good person you are meant to be. Strive to be an example by your love for everyone around you. Find your full potential. When all is said and done, write a song, a poem or book. Live, love, laugh and think of God—and then thank Him.

Tribute to a Father – Jim (May 7, 1997)

I want to write and thank you for all the things you did
To make my young life stable after rough years as a kid.
You took on quite a battle when you took on us three
Your life was never boring with Sandy, Mom and me.
Your days became a challenge, once we settled in
You called us "Jimmy's Girls" and said it with "that" grin.
When you died we were not mentioned in any word or form
I just wanted to thank you and take some time to mourn.
Thank you for a house to live in, and for good food to eat
Thank you for the clothes we wore and late-night movie treats.
Thank you for the "box seats" at the Cleveland Indian Games
For early morning fishing trips and boats caught in the rain.
Thanks for poached egg breakfasts, and "Hot Toddies" to cure colds
For "Indian Head" nickels, and stuffed animals to hold.
Thanks for allowances and curfews and homework to be done
For rules and regulations and the "right time" to have fun.
You were the closest to a Father us girls had ever had
And you know we cared about you and would have loved to call you Dad.
Thank you for the bunny and for the hamsters too
Thanks for "Pidge" and "Pepper," the place was quite a zoo.
I remember how you loved your back scratched late at night
Of course, I would just do it to stay up without a fight.
You struggled with our music and with our "Hippie" beads
With boys at crazy hours and our many sneaky deeds.

You saw us through the teen years, then gave away the bride
Our children called you "Papa," you wore the name with pride.
Then after the divorce, the title "Dad" would end
And with your jealous "daughter," I couldn't stay your friend.
You have an "only daughter," and she sure tells everyone
But please know you have two others whose love has gone unsung.
If you didn't know before this, you surely know it now
That we have always loved you, but we were not allowed.
And as the years went by, Dad, I came to understand
The times you made us crazy "you were doing the best you can."
A lot that's good about me I attribute to your care
Cause in the years that counted, you were the one right there.
When I take care of my yard I'll always think of you
And when I plant my garden I'll think of you then too.
And when I do my budget, I cannot help but grin
I learned so much from you and how proud you would have been.
Our God has a sense of humor, we're all a little strange
But that is not a problem, it's probably been arranged.
It's the end of life that matters, when we leave this world like you
People say you were a "good guy," and we all know that was true.
So, this is my little tribute to a man I knew with pride
I had to let my feelings out, not keep them locked inside.
I'll say goodbye for now, Dad, until we meet again
Thanks again for being my "Father" and my trusted friend.
And when I get to heaven, if I can pick a "Dad"
God knows that here on Earth, you were the best I ever had.

THE DOGWOOD

MAY 2003

Mothers' day without you
You've been gone a little while
I can think about you now
I can even wear a smile
We did so much together
We were close in many ways
We laughed, we cried, we shared so much
But that was another day
My dogwood tree is blooming
Of course, I think of you
You were so ill when it was planted
I prayed you'd both pull through
I'd brought you many dogwoods
And planted in your yard
But each one of them just faded
This one has thrived so far
I miss you, Mom, God knows I do
But it hurts still to remember
Your illness just before you left
Your angry words so hurtful
Your loss has tested all my strengths
And shaken my beliefs
I miss you more, as this hurt fades
Losing you was bittersweet

Summary: Brenda was born during the "Great Appalachian Storm," November 1950 (a cyclone that broke all records). Her mother suffered through a long and difficult labor at Saint Joseph's Hospital in Buckhannon, West Virginia. Nuns prayed for the young Baptist family. Brenda's mother was a schizophrenic and her father was a dangerous alcoholic. The illnesses of her parents were life-threatening, deeply scarring their daughters with abuse, fear and neglect. Brenda's first book "Snippets of Heaven" is like a mirror opposite of this one. It depicts her adventures on her grandparents' farm. The farm was a safe, happy place. This book, *Glimpses of Hell,* recalls stories of a dark, scary life under the "care" of her parents.

Bio: Brenda's entire life is in her poetry as there are well over 120 poems, to be published at some future date. Brenda is an avid exercise enthusiast. She enjoys golfing and shooting sporting clays, both of which she took up in her sixties. She has always enjoyed hiking, swimming, aerobic exercise and weight training. Sunshine and fresh air are her elixir. Most recently she has taken up hula hooping. She laughed so hard at herself when she started hooping at age 65. Laughing is as important as praying in her life, and God has a sense of humor.

Brenda's next book, about her three husbands, will be titled: *Three Shades of Black and White-Pieces of Purgatory*. It is filled with God's sense of humor and his many blessings. She has been married three times, in her words "to very different, exciting and interesting men. I learned so much from each of them and loved each of them deeply at some point in time. I was also blessed to be the mother of four wonderful children. My greatest heartbreak and loss was outliving two of them."

Melbalene and George 1943

Melbalene and George 1945

Sandy and Brenda 1953

Sandy and Brenda 1955

". . . we also speak of when we were suffering. We know that suffering can create endurance, endurance can create character, and character can create confidence. We are not ashamed to have this confidence, because God's love has been poured into our hearts by the Holy Spirit, who has given it to us." Romans 5:3-5

I want to dedicate this book to each and every person that is fighting their own demons, whether it be alcohol, drugs, abuse or neglect of family. I pray you seek help. I pray that you heal. I pray that you can become the person that even you can be proud of. God is there for you. Open your wounded and broken heart, let Him in.

www.ingramcontent.com/pod-product-compliance
Lightning Source LLC
Chambersburg PA
CBHW051922160426
43198CB00012B/1996